Crazy

Notes On and Off the Couch

Rob Dobrenski, PhD

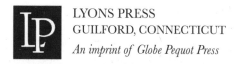
LYONS PRESS
GUILFORD, CONNECTICUT
An imprint of Globe Pequot Press

Lyons Press is an imprint of Globe Pequot Press.

ISBN 978-0-7627-7847-8

Text design: Sheryl P. Kober
Layout: Mary Ballachino
Project editor: Kristen Mellitt

The Library of Congress has previously catalogued an earlier (hardcover) edition as follows:

Dobrenski, Rob.
  Crazy : notes on and off the couch / Rob Dobrenski.
      p. cm.
  Summary: "An average day in the life of a psychologist is a frenetic one. A 9 a.m. appointment to help a woman manage a husband who won't take out the garbage (at least with pants on) quickly shifts to a session with a convicted rapist at 10 a.m. After talking with a child about his fears of school an hour later, the psychologist then meets with a therapist to deal with his own fears, followed by lunch with his socially-phobic colleague who's already had four martinis by 1 p.m. All this, and it's only Monday. Is it any wonder, then, that therapists are often depressed, anxious, and prone to panic attacks? Or that they take antipsychotics, self-medicate with booze, and struggle in their own relationships? Crazy is the story of how one mental health professional deals with his own personal problems and those of the people he treats. Part expos and part memoir, it reveals what therapists really think about their profession, their colleagues, their patients, and their own lives. "-- Provided by publisher.
  ISBN 978-0-7627-6483-9 (hardback)
  1. Dobrenski, Rob. 2. Psychologists--New York--Biography. 3. Psychology--Practice.
I. Title.
  BF109.D63A3 2011
  616.89'14092--dc22
  [B]

                                      2011013045

Printed in the United States of America

10 9 8 7 6 5 4 3 2 1

To every person who has emotionally suffered, who recognized and accepted that going it alone wasn't cutting it, who realized help from another was required, who stood up to the stigma of seeking professional assistance and went out to get it, and even to those who couldn't afford to do so but did something to improve: This book is for you.

crazy \ krā-zē \ adj. mentally deranged, especially as manifested in a wild or aggressive way

Oxford Dictionary

crazy \ krā-zē \ adj. experiencing any kind of emotional pain or distress, i.e., what we all grapple with as part of the human condition

Rob Dobrenski, PhD

CONTENTS

A Note to the Reader

The "inside" look you are about to read is based on my real-life experiences as both a graduate student and practicing psychologist. My story, in many ways, represents what nearly every mental health professional experiences at one time or another. Any shrink who tells you he or she can't relate to what is written here is incredibly guarded and private, which is one of the many reasons this book needed to be written.

Due to the extremely sensitive nature of the subject matter, I have taken artistic license to protect the identity of those involved (please see Disclaimer). Fortunately, the essence of the stories and their inherent messages is not lost with these changes. Even though what I describe here is a "day" in the life of a shrink, what you're really seeing is fifteen years' worth of experience, from my early training experiences to my current practice. These stories are symbolic of what mental health professionals do on a regular basis. So although you won't be able to put the timeline together like puzzle pieces, rest assured you're getting an inside glimpse into this world.

Psychologists have one of the greatest jobs on Earth: We help give our patients relief from mental and emotional pain. We listen and respond to psychological difficulties on an hourly basis, hear people share their deepest secrets. Day after day, week after week, we give wisdom, direction, advice, and perspective. Many people venerate us for this. A day in the life of a shrink is daunting, humbling, exciting, and, most often, incredibly gratifying as we sit with people from all walks of life. We meet many interesting people with fascinating, sometimes "edge-of-your seat" stories to tell.

Our workdays are actually quite frenetic. Sometimes the therapy hour is humorous and lighthearted, such as when we listen to a woman lament over her horrible date with a millionaire who insisted they dine at Taco Bell (and only from the value menu, of course). Other times it's serious and sobering, like when we need to help a teenager stop slicing her arms and legs. One hour we might be playing checkers with an eight-year-old as he talks about his feelings toward his dad; the next, we are filling out an admission form for a man who walks into the hospital, places a gun on the counter, and says, "Please help me."

And yet while we bask in the glow of giving people a better quality of life, letting people believe we are "mental health giants," we ourselves suffer. We're depressed and anxious; we battle with crippling panic attacks, OCD, and post-traumatic stress disorder. We take Zoloft, or worse, antipsychotics. We get God complexes and sometimes charge exorbitant fees. We drink too much and have horrible relationships. And sometimes we even have no clue what we are doing in the office! We love to believe that we are perhaps quirky, eccentric, maybe even neurotic, but certainly not *ill* (and yet sometimes we are). We sit in our offices, listening to people talk about themselves, helping in ways that often impact them for perhaps the rest of their lives, and yet we never let them know how screwed up we really are. In reality, we're just like them: crazy.

Welcome to this world.

DISCLAIMER

While this book includes anecdotes based on true events, several changes have been made to protect the identity of those involved. Such changes include—but are not limited to—altered names, dates, locations, genders, and ages. In addition, in several instances the individuals described are, in fact, composite characters created from experiences working with numerous patients and colleagues dealing with the same or similar issues. These steps are taken to protect client confidentiality in accordance with both ethical and legal guidelines.

PROLOGUE

As a twenty-four-year-old graduate student, I met with a patient I'll call Bill, who was a chronically depressed fifty-five-year-old man. Although Bill suffered from significant mood problems, he was consistently polite and personable. This allowed him to connect with and be liked by people quite easily, myself included. And even though I lacked experience—at that point in my training I had sat down with only a handful of patients—I assumed I could use my modicum of education to improve his quality of life.

While Bill's likability made the work enjoyable, after several months of therapy, I grew frustrated that we had made little progress as a therapeutic team. One day, however, there was a drastic shift in his mood.

"Guess what, Rob?" he said proudly. "I finally drove my car."

Normally morose, on this day Bill was happy, practically ecstatic, perhaps for the first time in years. This good news left me puzzled, however.

"What do you mean, you drove?" I asked. "Where? Up and down your driveway?"

"No, I mean the real deal. I drove all the way here with a friend, the whole three miles . . ."

"But—"

"I took the highway most of the ride until the traffic got too heavy . . ."

"How could you—"

". . . and then I turned off to drive the side roads through a couple of neighborhoods. I really picked up some speed there."

"Oh, Jesus . . ."

Most therapists would have been elated to learn that a patient who had been so depressed he often found it difficult to get out of bed before three in the afternoon had suddenly summoned enough courage to discard the safety of his routine. Bill had driven three miles along a tortuous highway and then continued for another mile through two busy school zones just to get a sense of his own independence. But I was not, in fact, elated by what I was now hearing. In fact, I didn't know what I felt.

It's not every day that a blind man drives himself to his therapy appointment, but there it was. And Bill wasn't just legally blind, as in someone who could navigate through life with the aid of heavy-duty contact lenses. No, Bill was *stone-cold blind*. He had been born with sight and had even driven a car—just not in years. Many, many years.

"I think I'm finally cured," he said after recounting further details of his misadventure. "Aren't you proud of me, Rob?"

Proud? I had to admit that "proud" wasn't the first word that came to mind. Shocked, yes. Puzzled, definitely. *Should I confront this behavior as unacceptable? Will he be offended or, even worse, depressed that I'm not pleased with his "progress"? What do I do? Thank God he can't see how fucking confused I must look.*

Depression can create an intense vulnerability in patients, and more often than not it's best for a psychologist to keep a mood buoyed whenever possible, especially with patients who chronically suffer. Emotions can change quickly, and Bill needed to keep a taste of happiness in his mouth. Although it was simply a barely educated guess at that point in my training, I rightly decided that his morale was the most important thing right then. Therefore I spoke to him in the gentlest, most therapeutic tone I could muster.

"Bill, you and I have been working together for a fairly long time now, and you've really had a tough go of things lately, so I love the fact that you're being more . . . active, and taking control of your life. That's a good thing. But I think you should ask your-self whether you've made an . . . appropriate choice here. Don't you think driving a car in your condition was a tad dangerous? You had to drive past two school zones with children continually darting in and out from between parked cars, and then there's the hospital and the retirement home on your way here. Would your friend have been able to tell you in time if someone cut in front of you, or if you had to stop short for another car?"

"Hey, Jim was on top of it all the way, and I have great reflexes. You know how they say that when you lose one sense, the others get stronger? Well, I can *feel* the car now, the flow, and I know exactly where to go."

Bill was directing his words at least three feet to my left, so his thesis about sensory ability was dubious at best.

"My senses are stronger now," he continued. "It's all good, really. See?" he said, as he held up a copy of the *Wall Street Journal*. "I can tell this is the *New York Times* just from the feel of it."

"Look, I think it's great that you're taking more risks," I said. "But we should discuss some other choices you might make to express your independence, actions that won't place anyone in jeopardy . . ."

As the session continued, I handed out affirming statements while stressing that having driven once, Bill no longer had to prove himself again. But, to be honest, as I was delivering what any student would have, a confused and naive voice played in my head:

How the hell did this happen? We've been working our asses off for months, and nothing has worked until this "cure" comes along? Can I have him committed for being a danger to himself and others? Should I? Why didn't my professors go over DWBD (Driving While Blind Disorder) in class? Jesus, he better have plans to walk home after the session, or I'll have no idea what to say.

Bill smiled. Not at me, but at the plant a few feet to my right. He was so pleased with himself. And then a thought hit me, hard. It was a cognition that I'd never put any serious meaning behind, and one that rendered me guilt-stricken for weeks afterward: *Oh my God, this guy is fucking crazy.*

During the early portion of my training, some of my classmates and I met for dinner and a discussion about why we were in the graduate program, and what we hoped to accomplish in our careers. While many people believe that we become shrinks simply to learn how to provide ourselves with free therapy and to resolve our own childhood issues, the reality is that most mental health practitioners are reasonably altruistic people who want to help others. And, if we are lucky, we may make a decent living in the process. This was at least the most common response given by the new graduate students. However, in what seemed like an improbable coincidence, my classmate Pete and I grew up having heard the same name for shrinks—"feelings doctors"—which is what had drawn us into the field.

When I was about ten years old I ended up at the doctor's office, probably to be treated for one of my innumerable tree-climbing accidents. In the same suite as my pediatrician, a man sat crying in the waiting room. In fact, he was sobbing with his face in his hands. He didn't seem to be in any physical pain, so his tears puzzled me. "Mom, why would an adult cry at the doctor's?" I asked.

"Robert, people have problems," she answered. "That man might need help with whatever is making him sad. He's probably seeing the other doctor who's an expert in that."

"Adults see a doctor when they feel sad?" I asked incredulously.

"Sometimes. Many people need to see someone who is a professional in making people not sad. That's okay. You can ask for help when your feelings are broken. The feelings doctors are very, very important people."

This experience stayed with me for a few reasons. Even at a young age I was interested in the healing professions. Throughout my childhood, there never was a time that I didn't imagine myself becoming a doctor, dentist, phlebotomist, or some other health-related artisan. Part of it may have been the fact that they all drove very nice cars and that people seemed to regard them with palpable reverence. "I have to wait three weeks to see Dr. Goldtouch? I need her *now!*" I imagined it must have been a wonderful experience to be in such demand. But a "feelings doctor" was something new to me. And the crying man looked to be in far more pain than anyone else in the waiting room. Could emotions hurt more than a broken leg?

I was still in the waiting room—we all know how sadistic doctors can be when it comes to making their patients wait well past their appointment time—when the man emerged from the Feelings Doctor's office, and I noticed he seemed better. Not in the "all smiles with a Band-Aid and lollipop" way, but he wasn't crying anymore, and he had the slightest hint of happiness as he shook the hand of the Feelings Doctor. It seemed as if the therapist had had a huge impact on the man, perhaps the most of any of the providers there that day.

I thought about the man and what my mother had told me, and I immediately bought into what she had described as the philosophy of a shrink. It made sense to me: People have problems, plain and simple, and it's okay to get help with them. Of course, every doctor I had ever met seemed godlike to me. What they said was gospel. They gave you a pill and you felt better. They told you to not eat that green paste in the garage and you suddenly didn't feel sick anymore. And even though I thought they were lying when they swore a colossal needle would prevent rubella, they were spot-on.

This perceived omniscience created in me an assumption that doctors were exempt from the issues of "regular" people. As a psychologist-in-training who had grown up in a reasonably healthy and happy home, I assumed that I might have at least some problems as an adult, but I also believed that my issues would be more manageable than other people's. My classmates certainly seemed well put together, so it was easy to buy into the notion that mental health doctors, even ones in training, had fewer mental issues than most, or at least knew how to solve them better than other people did. "Doctor = healthy, patient = sick" was my initial working model. And when my classmate Pete told me how *his* parents suggested that shrinks were a special brand of human, I immediately connected with him.

A few weeks after Bill's roadway epiphany, I began meeting up with Pete for what is known in the field as "peer supervision." This is a time to discuss our work and help each other deal with difficult issues that invariably arise. Throughout graduate training you always have your professors to lean on, but there's something refreshing about discussing issues with someone who's just as green as you are. Psychology students have yet to be clouded by years of doing things a certain way, and because psychology and therapy are fluid sciences, there are always new ways of viewing things that can help to advance the field.

I had planned to speak with Pete about Bill's treatment. At this point Bill was still riding high after his near demolition derby, and I was still greatly conflicted. Part of me was pleased about the improvement in his mood, while another part of me felt professionally derelict in not knowing how to respond to something that could endanger dozens of people. And yet another part of me wondered if I had said something to cause this near catastrophe that was doubling as a therapeutic breakthrough.

Like most graduate students in the field of psychology, Pete looked very "normal" at first glance. Those in mental health often appear to have above-average social skills and can engage others in conversation quite well. They make excellent eye contact and are often incredibly good listeners. They nod a lot to show you they are paying attention while you speak. The message conveyed is, "See how confident and comfortable I am talking with you? I'm like this all the time, even outside of the office. Share your problems with me and I'll help you with them." Pete was this and more in both the classroom and therapy space. Not only did he care about helping people, but he was also a voracious student. He wanted to know every theorist's take on the subconscious mind and have a complete command of all 900-something pages of the *Diagnostic and Statistical Manual of Mental Disorders, 4th Edition* (DSM-IV). He took extra care to be an excellent statistician should he ever decide to go into research. Most graduate students who aren't planning on an academic career see much of the reading, papers, and dissertations as simply necessary evils, a means to an end. They simply want to get in there and heal. Pete wanted more than that; he wanted to know and embrace everything the field had to offer.

Walking down a shop-lined street while discussing my experience with Bill, we bumped into one of Pete's own patients. When this happens, it can be quite awkward for both therapist and patient, especially if particularly intimate thoughts and feelings have been revealed in session. And, as Murphy's Law would have it, the patient had a young woman in tow.

I'll call the man Don, who, now standing two feet in front of us outside of a grocery store, smiled a big grin of recognition. "Pete!" he screamed at an unnecessary volume.

Therapist Rule 1: Unless a client/patient addresses you, do not make any form of contact.

It is the therapist's responsibility to ensure clients are not unnecessarily made to feel awkward or uncomfortable outside of the office. Knowing Pete, I assumed that he would handle this situation with razor-sharp skill. Instead, he just clumsily mumbled, "Hi, Don. Um, how are you?"

"Great, great! Just great! What are you up to?"

Therapist Rule 2: Do not unnecessarily disclose excessive personal information, especially outside of the office.

"I'm just, uh, just going for a walk in the park with my colleague, Rob," he barely stammered out. It was strange seeing

Pete look so socially awkward. Granted, I'd only known him for a few weeks, and I hadn't seen him interact with all that many people, but the discrepancy between his interactions with me, his knowledge of the field, and what was unfolding here was puzzling.

"This is my new lady, Darla," Don said, pointing to the woman next to him.

I looked at Pete, who was now flushed, and I started entertaining unlikely possibilities as to why Pete was showing early signs of a nervous breakdown. *It's just a client; what's the big deal? Could Pete be having sex with Darla? Or Don?*

To fill in the unusually long pregnant pause, I decided that I should at least contribute something. "Hello, Darla," I said, extending my hand.

"Darla already knows about us, Pete," Don explained. *So it's true. Pete's in bed with Don!*

"I just told her about our last session, in fact."

Oh, she knows that Don is a client. Not nearly as interesting, but at least it's on the level.

"Pete," Don continued, "could you please, *please* confirm what I told you last time? You know, about my manhood? My exact words? She doesn't believe me."

Therapist Rule 3: Do not engage in therapeutic services outside of the office or prearranged setting.

Pete had to have known this, but as the beads of sweat became clearly visible on his brow, I considered the possibility that he might spontaneously combust, leaving me, Don, and Darla to explain to his parents how their son had died.

Eventually Pete spoke. "I don't think that's appropriate, Don, especially in this setting."

"I'd like to hear about that," I said, almost reflexively. Pete shot me a look of both terror and rage.

"Yeah, Pete," Don and Darla simultaneously confirmed.

Nearly paralyzed with embarrassment and fear, Pete took a deep breath, not unlike what one does before announcing at his first twelve-step meeting that he is an alcoholic. "You made it a point to say that your penis, when 'engorged,' can split a woman in two, rendering her your sex slave for all time. At which point you dropped your pants to give me a 'sneak preview' of what your next 'lottery winner' would be experiencing." Pete hung his head in humiliation, possibly considering murder/suicide.

Wow. "Um, that's one fine penis you must have there, Don," I said. If there was any truth to what Pete had just revealed, any at all, Don deserved to be praised.

"You said it, Rob," said Don. "See, Darla, I told you!"

"All right, all right, I believe you. Let's leave these two to their walk, it's getting chilly," said Darla.

"Thanks, Pete," said Don. "I'll see you next week."

As Don and Darla walked away, I looked at Pete, who was now slightly bent over, holding his stomach, taking deep breaths. Were those tears I saw?

"Pete, what the hell is going on?"

"I . . . I get panic attacks. I have social anxiety."

How could this be? "What—you? I don't get it; you've never seemed anything but incredibly confident."

"It's not all the time," Pete said, who was now on all fours trying to collect himself, wiping his nose with his sleeve. "Therapy has helped decrease the frequency of attacks. And I take beta-blockers, which of course I fucking forgot to do this morning."

"You take *medication* for this?" I asked, astonished that "one of us" was on psychotropic drugs. It would ultimately take years for me to realize the extent of medication use within the community of mental health professionals.

"Yes," he said, as his panting slowly subsided. "And some other stuff that you'll never know about."

Other stuff? Like cocaine? Heroin? Nyquil?

"And by the way," he whimpered, "if you tell anyone about this, I'll kill you."

And then it dawned on me. *Oh my God, Pete is fucking crazy . . .*

It was strange spending time with Pete after that day, especially in public.

What drug is he currently on? I would wonder. *Does anyone else notice that slight twitch in his eye when he has to order at restaurants? Did he smoke pot to relax a bit? Something stronger? How on Earth can he do his job when he's so freaked out all the time?*

Most graduate school programs in clinical psychology are female-dominated, so Pete and I comprised the majority of the male student body. However, when Pete got a girlfriend—after what I had seen, how they had basic conversations without him jumping out of a window was beyond me—I was alone more often than I would have liked. I had other friends in school but no one I truly connected with, so I started thinking about whether a female companion would be a nice addition to my life in graduate school.

That question was answered when I met Janet in the fall of the next academic year. Bar none, she was the best-looking student in the history of graduate studies, foreign or domestic. A mere twenty-four years of age, she had broken up with her boyfriend of two years just days after she'd enrolled in the clinical psychology program. I had a crush that teetered on obsession the moment I saw her ragingly beautiful red hair. She was tall, thin, and could easily have been a runway model if she didn't want to be a shrink. I often wondered how any man on the planet would be able to have her as his therapist without fantasizing about her. Never before (or since) had I ever believed in the notion of Love at First Sight, but when Janet came into focus, I simply *knew.* She was the one. As a teenager, when I'd thought about what life might look like in ten or twenty years, she was the woman I envisioned. It was as if the film *Weird Science* had come to life and someone had created this physical specimen just for me. Or maybe the gods had simply decreed that this was the moment I was to meet my soul mate. Something clicked, and I made a conscious decision to form an indelible bond with her.

Like most young men I was hyperfocused on her physical beauty, and I let my hormones dictate my actions. Within hours of her arrival on campus, I asked her out. She accepted, subtly noting that it would be fun to "have a distraction while recovering from a breakup." But Mr. Rebound would have none of that. Instead of some casual fun a few times a week, I was prepared on a daily basis to win her over and make her mine: dinners, movies, walks around town. Flowers, candy, love notes—anything and everything to prove that coming on too strong was exactly what women love. Pairing that with my unique ability to hear *I love you* when a person says "I can't get involved with someone at this point in my life," created a perfect recipe for disaster.

A few months into my psychotic lovefest, Janet dumped me. I had arrived at her apartment with a six-foot-tall teddy bear holding a sign that said MY HEART DOES EVERYTHING BUT "SHRINK" WHEN I'M WITH YOU. I was so dumb that I was actually shocked when it happened. *But we were meant to be together! Didn't you see* Weird Science?!

"Rob, I told you what this was when we first went out," she said. "I never meant to mislead you."

And she hadn't; I was just young and stupid. Quite stupid, actually.

I left her apartment in the pouring rain, hoping to be struck by lightning. But no luck. And when she got back together with her ex a few weeks later, I began looking for the closest train under which I could throw myself.

For the first few weeks I ate very little and slept even less. I couldn't concentrate on school or friends, and I isolated myself in my small apartment. I would take the few photos I had of Janet and me and color our hair with a gray crayon, then would cry all over them at the realization that we would never grow old together. I drank a lot of beer and cried incessantly while doing so, with such volume that the salty tears would begin to mix with the foaming antidepressant. I had literally created a new, depressive cocktail. Beer and Tears. And while many of us at some point lose what we believe is our true love, time was not serving me well like it did for some. It was as if because I had decided that things were *supposed* to be one way, I refused to move forward in the face of evidence to the contrary. And because the feelings were so raw, an emotional burn that covered my entire body, productive introspection was virtually impossible.

A few more months went by, and I wasn't improving. Seeing Janet and her boyfriend at parties made me want to light all three of us on fire. I tore up the photos I had colored with gray crayon, and then actually ate one of the shreds in an attempt to preserve our bond.

I started snapping at people, to the point where a professor asked me if I had "something personal" going on. When I told her the truth, that I had been dipping my pen in the corporate ink and got jilted, she suggested that I see a therapist. This idea had occurred to me after I consumed two bottles of red wine in one night, but I resisted. *This is normal; I'm just hurt. I'll get over it. Time heals all wounds*, and lots of other platitudes that for some reason didn't apply to me. Students were encouraged to be in treatment during their training, and my professor said it would be like killing two birds with one stone. "You know the phrase 'know thyself'? Well, here's your chance to really understand the miserable person that you are."

My treatment provider, "Carol," was a middle-aged therapist with spectacles and a serious, analytical look, even when smiling. *A classic shrink*, I thought, and I wondered what I would look like in twenty years, sitting in my therapist's chair, probably still crying over Janet.

She asked me if I knew why my reaction to a fairly common occurrence was so strong, and I admitted that I had no idea. She then asked if I ever thought about killing myself, a question shrinks typically ask patients who are suffering from depression. But hearing the question gave me pause. *Kill myself? Is that what I wanted: to be dead?* I pictured myself lying in a morgue with a tag on my foot and a photo of Janet in my cold hand and realized that no, that wasn't quite right.

"I've thought about killing myself," I told Carol, "but I don't want to be dead. I just want to stop feeling this way, and sometimes that seems like the only option."

"I see," Carol said, the way a lot of shrinks do when they're thinking a few questions ahead. "And how long have you been feeling this way?"

"For about four months," I said. "It's hard because I see her almost every day, and I've always done better with an 'out of sight, out of mind' approach for breakups."

"All right," she said. "Let's see if we can help you process the grief. But I wonder if you'd be served well with an antidepressant, too."

Was I biologically out of whack now? Had my serotonin levels simply fallen to unacceptable levels? Was that what was stopping me from moving on? And why couldn't I make a life worth living outside of the context of a relationship that never really existed?

"You really think I need medication?" I asked—partially wanting her to say *No, that's actually a stupid idea; you're far too normal!* while another piece of me was excited about the idea of something, anything, that might seal up what felt like a gigantic hole in my torso.

"I do," she said, with a warm smile that exuded confidence. *Trust me on this one,* her look implied. *It will help.*

The few friends who were able to force me to talk about what was going on saw that I wasn't making enough headway with just dialogue. It happens that way sometimes. Sometimes people reach a point where they need something to kick-start their biochemistry. I was at that point. Plenty of other people get there and simply continue to struggle, but I was defeated. I wasn't able to fight anymore.

One week later I had a prescription for Zoloft from a local psychiatrist in my hand. Fifty milligrams once per day in the morning, preferably with food. *At least I'll only have to admit to myself that my brain is broken in the a.m.*

It was then, standing outside the psychiatrist's office, that I thought about Bill. *He needed, absolutely needed to drive that car. That was how he was going to overcome his depression. He knew of no other way.* And Pete. *He couldn't deal with other people outside of the therapy room. He's paralyzed without beta-blockers and probably heroin and who knows what else.* And me. *I can't handle a loss like this. I don't know how to cope without help.* Now that I had my own problems to deal with, I realized how naive I'd been for being judgmental about Bill and Pete. I couldn't even run my *own* life, let alone help them with theirs.

Bill.

Pete.

Me.

We're all the same in many ways.

Oh my God . . . I'm fucking crazy too.

9 a.m.
Seeing the World through Black-Painted Glasses

When Bill, the Stevie Wonder of the highway, first came into our school's clinic, I engaged him in what is known as cognitive therapy (CT). Over the past fifty years CT has supplanted traditional Freudian psychoanalysis as the treatment of choice for major depression, given a large body of research that suggests it works more quickly (making it more cost-effective) and has longer-lasting results. Some studies have demonstrated that CT is as effective as medication in the treatment of depression.

CT is predicated on the notion that conscious thought is the largest influence on both mood and behavior. CT works to help clients identify and modify thought patterns that are leading to depressive states. Therapists provide clients with tools and strategies to help them alter maladaptive thought patterns. This brings about a change in mood and an alleviation of symptoms.

Because it is a skills-based therapy, the goal of CT is to educate clients to become their own therapists. Thus, clients are taught how to evaluate the way their thought patterns are impacting them rather than simply being told that the way they think is "wrong" or "dysfunctional." This approach not only empowers clients but also validates the fact that the way they have been approaching their life is the best they've been able to do thus far.

Some research suggests that neophyte therapists can be as effective using CT as seasoned clinicians, independent of therapeutic approach. I clearly wasn't a subject in this study because I was a horrible therapist as a student. Watching videotapes of Dr. Pete effortlessly coast through sessions only to vomit later in his wastebasket not only confused but frustrated me no end. Part of the problem was that I was so eager to help a client see his faulty logic that I simply spoon-fed it to him rather than let him come to his conclusions based on the tools I was "teaching" him.

When Bill became depressed it wasn't due to losing his sight; nor was it the loss of his ability to drive. In fact, there wasn't any precipitating factor, which isn't uncommon in depressive episodes. People who haven't been depressed make this assumption all the time: What does *she* have to be depressed about? She's got it all— money, a great job, a loving family, etc. The reality is that many people can't pinpoint why or how or what they are even depressed about. And yet their mood is down, sleep is off, appetite is either ravenous or nonexistent, unfounded guilty feelings are through the roof, and sometimes suicidal thoughts are part of the depressive package. For Bill, spending most of the day in bed was the norm, with self-talk (cognitions) that was generally self-deprecating: *You're worthless, your family hates you, you can't do anything right.* This would occur despite the fact that Bill's family did, in fact, love him, and that he was an active member in the blind community, helping the handicapped adjust to lifestyle changes due to their lack of sight.

And yet something wasn't clicking for him. "Bill, tell me about the last time you worked with a person who recently lost his sight," I asked during one session.

"It didn't go so well. The man wouldn't take to the assignments to use his hands more thoroughly as I had instructed him."

"And when that happened, what went through your mind?"

"That he'll never get better. That I'll never be able to help anyone because I'm worthless."

Now a good therapist would help Bill to understand how these thoughts might be considered cognitive distortions—subtle skews in perception that bring about a depressed mood. The therapist would then teach him to evaluate those thoughts on his own so that he would know what to do if and when those cognitions emerged again. However, Bill didn't have a "good" therapist; he had me. As a young doctoral student I was particularly impatient when it came to allowing the process to unfold as it should. My approach was simply to tell Bill how wrong he was in his thinking.

"No, Bill, no! You don't know that he'll *never* get better; that's what we call fortune-telling. And you've helped plenty of people before! Saying you won't be able to help 'anyone' is a form of all-or-nothing thinking. You're basically saying that you suck completely simply because this guy didn't take to the techniques right away. Do you see how fucked up that is?"

When Bill's mood didn't improve I myself felt depressed. As part of our training the students and professors would discuss cases (this was mandated by state law, as none of the students were licensed psychologists). When I shared my therapy failures regarding Bill with my professor, whom I'll call Dr. Charles, I actually adopted Bill's thought process: "Bill's not getting better. This is never going to work. I suck. I'm going to be a horrible psychologist." If I'd had a glass of red wine in the classroom I would have chugged it on the spot to cope with the raging incompetence I felt.

"Rob," Dr. Charles said very calmly and patiently, as a seasoned psychologist might (essentially he was everything I was not), "both you and Bill have to understand that your work together is a *process*, not an *event*. You both want results in a New York minute. The reality is that this will likely work for him, and fairly quickly, but you both are oozing with cognitive distortions now. Tell me, in retrospect, what you think you did wrong?"

I could practically taste the wine. "I . . . didn't use any sort of Socratic questioning. I simply pointed out the flaws in his thinking without helping him to develop a sense of cognitive discretion. I then essentially demanded that he see things from my point of view." *See the proof? I'm terrible! Are you happy now, you merciless warlock?!*

"Good. Now let's go over how you could approach this issue with him again."

During the ensuing weeks and months I learned how to work with Bill. When the next student in Bill's training program struggled, I worked with him in a much different way.

"Bill, let's try this again. I think I came on a little strong the last time this topic came up. Tell me what went through your mind when your student didn't take to the assignments."

"It was just like last time," Bill said. "He'll never get better. I'm worthless because I can't help anyone."

"Those are powerful thoughts. And what emotions followed from that?"

"I feel depressed, down, worthless."

"Exactly. But let's take a closer look at the two thoughts you mentioned. Have you ever had a client who initially didn't succeed or thrive in your program but ultimately improved?"

"Well, sure," Bill said. "Sometimes the clients are too overwhelmed with their handicap to move forward, and they need some time."

"I see. And how often does something like that happen?"

"I would say, for the group, like three-quarters of the time."

"That often? So in fairness to you, is it truly accurate to say, based on your agency's history, that he'll *never* get better?"

A short pause. "No, I suppose not."

"Do you remember that list of cognitive distortions I gave you? The ones that tend to negatively alter our mood?"

"The list you told me to carry in my pocket at all times? Yes, I remember. Fortune-telling, right?"

"You tell me," I said, with a growing confidence in both of us that I knew he would hear.

"Yes. The reality is that while it's possible he won't get better, the odds are that he will if I give him a fair amount of time."

"And how do you feel when you say that?"

"Not great, but a little better."

"That's a start. We're getting somewhere."

And we were. Bill learned how to challenge his thoughts and replace them with more-balanced, factually accurate thoughts. Theoretically his mood should have buoyed significantly because he was telling himself all the right things. And yet he wasn't improving to either of our satisfaction. His mood was slightly better, yes, and he spent less time in bed. But he was still depressed much of the time. He needed something more. And weeks later, after the NASCAR for the Blind adventure, he elucidated it for me.

"Rob, it's possible that I could get my sight back someday; the doctors say it could possibly be treated. I've come to realize I don't feel complete without my sight. Even though I tell my blind clients that this type of thinking is bullshit, that seeing isn't necessary to be happy, I still feel it. Driving was a huge part of my life and I miss it. It made me feel worthwhile because when I was driving, I thought about myself, my family, and my life, and I put all the pieces together. It was my therapy and it brought me great joy. It's when I felt whole. I needed to know, really *know* what it was like to be behind the wheel again. And the great feeling? It hasn't left."

Sometimes clients realize much later what the depression was about, so this revelation didn't come as a complete surprise to me.

"Was it stupid?" Bill asked. "Did I endanger people? We know the answers to those questions. Would I do it again? I don't think so, but the reality is that driving that car was the best intervention I could have had."

Right or wrong, better or worse, Bill needed a behavioral component to make everything come together. Changing his cognitive patterns was helpful, but he needed something outside of his thoughts. He needed action. This is why many therapists who practice CT are actually using cognitive-*behavioral* therapy, or CBT. It's the mix of changes, thoughts, and actions that packs the most therapeutic punch.

It may seem strange and sound like some visual cliché you see in a film, where the handicapped person overcomes tremendous obstacles to achieve a goal that changes his life, but there you have it. Bill and I worked together for a few more weeks to talk more about his now-remitted depression, and how he would handle things should he have a relapse. Per my insistence, this plan involved no driving until the sight issue had been resolved.

"Oh, I'll be back if it comes to that," Bill said with a smile. "You can be sure of it."

Dr. Charles taught me how to methodically educate a client on how to be his own therapist. Bill showed me that sometimes extreme measures are required for unorthodox problems. And my glass of wine tasted so much better as a "reward for a job well done," per Dr. Charles, than as an anti-incompetence drug.

It seemed strange when Dr. Charles credited me for the success of Bill's treatment. "You got him to the point where he needed to be. You helped him see what he needed to do." I didn't understand that logic at all and, at times, still question it. Bill could have gotten to that point out of sheer frustration whether I was in his life or not. "Or maybe he took action *because* of the lack of punch you were initially bringing," countered Dr. Charles. "Although it's only a correlation, the fact remains that he improved while he was under your care. For that you should be commended."

Dr. Charles saw me as oozing with potential. In retrospect I think he saw my low frustration tolerance as a personal challenge. I wanted people to get better, and quickly. He knew that these things took time and that I needed to embrace that fact if I was going to be any good at my craft. He also impressed upon me the concept of empathy:

"Empathy is the most significant tool a therapist has in his arsenal. Note, however, that this is not the same as sympathy or feeling sorry for someone. Sympathy is when you ask yourself, 'How would I feel if this was happening to me,' and you experience certain hypothetical emotions. Empathy is much more powerful. Empathy is trying to get into others' shoes to feel what they feel. You don't necessarily ignore your own emotions, but your goal is to try to be in their unique experience, in their psychology. When you are truly empathic, you feel connected to the client and attached to his or her experience. In turn, a client feels understood, accepted, and validated. Then he is open to hearing a fresh opinion, a new perspective, or a unique approach to solving a problem. Empathy is the glue that holds the therapy experience in place."

It is easy to empathize with certain types of people and issues—a grieving widow, for example, or a person who becomes depressed after being laid off from a job that provided for a family. Through a general sense of caring for the human condition, most of us can convey a strong sense of empathy for these clients.

Not all problems easily adapt to the empathic experience, however, and Dr. Charles knew this. Therefore, he volunteered me as a therapist in an off-campus research project that would put me to the test. The study was examining the use of empathy as a therapeutic tool. I was assigned to an African-American man in his early fifties, whom I'll call Scott, who was grappling with dysthymic disorder (a long-term, low-intensity depression). It is often described by clients as a "case of the blahs" that can't be shaken off.

Scott was six-foot-four, disheveled, overweight, and constantly perspiring. He began many of his sentences with an F-bomb and arrived for his sessions in T-shirts that were too tight for his abdomen, and white sneakers with black socks. His hands were always very clammy, but he insisted on a handshake every time he entered the therapy room. He was easily the brunt of many people's jokes.

Scott desperately needed to take better care of himself. He suffered from hypertension, high cholesterol, and diabetes. This isn't unheard of for people in depressive conditions. They lose interest in many things, including their self-care and their health. While Scott labeled his focus areas of therapy as "to get better with people" and "be with a family," my hope was that working together would allow him to make better food choices and begin an exercise program. How strange that was, given the fact that I couldn't have cared less about my own health while Janet's image was indelibly tattooed in my mind.

Clients who are part of experimental therapies are often required to consent to their sessions being audio- and/or video-taped. This allows for the dialogue to be transcribed and studied, and can also serve as a training tool for student therapists. Scott and I used audiotape, in part simply because I have horrible technical skills and couldn't operate a video camera or a tripod. As part of the research protocol, we used the first session to better understand and develop his goals for treatment. After the session, I met with Dr. Charles to review the tape:

Rob: *Scott, I'd like to know more about what you mean when you say "be with a family" as one of your goals.*

Scott: *I've been with a woman for about twelve years, but we're not married. She can't have any more children.*

Rob: *So you have children?*

Scott: *No, she has one child. I guess I'm a stepfather of sorts—a pretty good one, actually.*

Rob: *But are you saying that you'd like to have biological children?*

Scott: *Fuck, yeah—who wouldn't?*

Rob: *Okay, so does that mean that you will break up with your partner to find someone who can have kids?*

Scott: *No, fuck no, I love her. Her daughter is a virgin, so when the time comes we'll just use her for my seed.*

Stop. Rewind. Replay. Stop.

"What the hell is he talking about?" asked Dr. Charles.

"I think you need to listen to more."

Dr. Charles stared at me with a combination of confusion and suspicion, and then pressed PLAY.

Rob: *I see. Wait . . . what?*

Scott: *Her daughter is fourteen, and a virgin.*

Rob: *And?*

Scott: *And what?*

Rob: *And what does that have to do with your "seed"?*

Scott: *My partner and I agreed that when her daughter turns eighteen, I'll impregnate her and she'll have my baby.*

Rob: *Um . . . I see.*

Stop. Rewind. Replay. Stop.

"Jesus," said Dr. Charles, shuddering. "What do you think?"

"I think it's creepy. They're mentally grooming her to be the mother of this guy's child."

"What happens next? Just fill me in."

"I know I'm supposed to be asking about his goals, but I was afraid that they might be about sexually abusing her," I said. "I asked who else knew about this, and he said no one, just him and his partner. The girl doesn't know yet, and when she turns eighteen, if she doesn't want to do it, they won't try to force anything on her. They are simply going to ask for her to be a surrogate. Is that legal?"

"It doesn't sound like they're doing anything illegal. It's a bit bizarre, but probably not against the law."

"It's more than bizarre, it's scary to me."

"Hmmm," said Dr. Charles, and he rubbed his bearded chin in that clichéd therapist way. "It's like an arranged marriage, like in Eastern cultures."

"No, it's like an arranged fuck, like in fucked-up cultures."

"Let's look at this. This man—you don't like him?"

"I wouldn't say that. There are things about him that I don't like," I said.

"Okay, that's fine. It's not possible to like everything about everyone you work with. But what, specifically, do you not like about him?"

"Dr. Charles, there's a lot. I don't like that he doesn't take any pride in his health, or his appearance, for that matter. He's somewhat crude. No, very crude, and he's mentally screwing a fourteen-year-old girl until she's of age, and she just happens to be the daughter of his girlfriend."

"Okay, now think about the study, think about empathy. What is this man experiencing?"

"Horniness?"

"Rob, get off of your high horse and use your brain for a second."

"All right," I said, sighing. "Fine. I . . . I don't know."

"Then instead of simply judging, go back in there next session and find out more about what he is experiencing. Find something in him to love, anything at all. It could be the way he feels about kids, a pet, even a tree. See something in him that is lovable or endearing. This will help you to see him as a whole person, not just a mental pedophile."

If "loving everyone" were a disorder, Dr. Charles would need the highest dose of medication possible to treat it. Possibly electro-convulsive therapy.

When Scott came back the following week, I was determined to do more listening and less judging. When Dr. Charles and I played the tape after that session, this is what we heard:

Rob: *Scott, let's talk more about family, and why you want it so much.*

Scott: *Fuck, man, you don't want a family?*

Rob: *I don't know, to be honest. But even if I did, I want to know what is appealing to you about it.*

Scott: *I was always a fat kid. I never had many friends. People made fun of me. My mom and dad were real good to me, though. I could always defend myself because of my size, but it still fucking hurt, you know? To be made fun of for being fat? My mom and dad could see that it hurt me, and they didn't always know what to do, but every time, every fucking time, man, I could count on them to take me out to the park or to the toy store, to buy me a soda or a pack of gum. Sometimes we'd just watch TV together and have popcorn, but we'd be together and I'd be safe. Fucking safe, man. My mom always said, "Being a family man is the best kind of man." And I just knew that I should be a dad, a good dad. When they passed, it hurt, and I only had my girlfriend. I don't know how I got lucky enough to even get her; she's a real sweet lady.*

Rob: *You don't want to marry her?*

Scott: *She'd already been married and doesn't want to do that again, said that it's just a piece of paper. I guess I understand that. And she knows I want a kid.*

Rob: *If she can't have children, why don't you adopt?*

Scott: *Rob, do you think a black couple, unmarried, with hardly any money, can adopt a kid? You might be getting a degree, but you are pretty naive.*

Rob: *I'm sorry, I shouldn't have assumed like that. You're right, that was naive. Sadly, it's something I've become quite good at.*

Scott: *She doesn't want me to leave her for someone else, so she said that we'll see if her daughter would be willing to be my surrogate when the time comes. I know it's not normal, but it's all I can think of right now.*

Dr. Charles stopped the tape. "How do you feel about all of that?"

"I feel like an asshole for being so judgmental. I labeled him as a freak, but he's just someone struggling to find something that will make him happy."

"I don't think that labeling him was an abnormal thing to do; I was thrown off as well at first. That doesn't make it right, but it's part of the job sometimes. Did you feel any empathy this second time around?"

"I felt depressed, sort of hopeless for Scott," I said.

"That sounds like empathy to me. Maybe we'll make a psychologist out of you yet," he said with a goofy yet encouraging smile.

"Great," I said, not hiding my sarcasm. "What about Scott?"

"You're going to figure out a way to help him get through these emotions. If he can sense that you're no longer naive and that you understand what he is experiencing, he'll be open to help. Really listen to his words. Paraphrase them back to him; let him know you're trying to walk in his shoes. Show him that you're connected to him."

Scott and I were very different people. Empathy, therefore, was both a challenge and a necessity.

Scott wasn't like Bill in a few important ways: He didn't need to have his thoughts and perceptions directly challenged, nor did he have to take a life-altering step to alleviate his depression. But Scott needed to feel understood, to have his world validated. Over the weeks Dr. Charles heard changes when he listened to the tape:

Scott: Fuck, it's like, I know there are other options. Hell, there's one right in front of me.

Rob: So it's not that you have to go with the "sperm and egg" issue— that there is another way? Have I got that?

Scott: Right. I've got a daughter already; I just need to embrace it more.

Rob: Right. Be a good dad to the kid that's already here. Be a father to who needs you?

Scott: Exactly. Why do I have to be a biological father to be a dad?

Rob: *I don't think you do. Do you?*

Scott: *No. I don't have to. Maybe that's the way I would have it if things went perfectly for me, but that's not the way it is.*

Rob: *So you're saying, "If I could have had a biological child, great. But if not, I can still be a great dad."*

Scott: *Yeah, yeah. You get it, right?*

Rob: *I get it.*

"So where is this all going?" asked Dr. Charles during our weekly meeting.

"He needed to see for himself that the family he wanted was already there," I said. "He's a happier person because of it. His daughter actually makes him go jogging with her."

"Is he done with therapy?"

"Not yet. But he's close."

"So how did you do it? How did change come about?"

"To be honest, I don't think I know for sure. I know I listened, asked questions, paraphrased his statements to be sure I understood, and just went along for the ride."

"Not bad," said Dr. Charles. "Is that all good mental health practice is?"

I thought about this for a minute before responding, thinking about people like Bill, others with intractable psychiatric conditions, and the limits of the field of mental health.

"Sometimes," I finally said. "It depends on the disorder and the person. Some people need medication, some need cognitive therapy, and some need something else. For Scott, though, what we're doing seems to be all that he needs."

"Depressive disorders tend to be recurrent. What if it comes back?"

"Then I suppose he'll be back," I said, confident that I could help Scott should he need someone again.

"Dobrenski, you're a genius," he said.

Scott completed his therapy and didn't need to return, at least during my tenure in graduate school. And I never forgot Dr. Charles's tutelage when it came to treating depression. He used his well-honed empathy skills to appreciate my plight as an ignorant student, and simultaneously taught me to be a more empathic clinician. If only he had really referred to me as a genius.

10 a.m.
Panic and Dr. Pete

At the time I first considered writing a book I was a mildly popular blogger who wrote quirky, offbeat stories about mental health on a website I had founded, called ShrinkTalk.net. My goal at the time was to show a real, behind-the-scenes look at what happened in the shrink's office, in hopes that I could debunk some myths and stigmas about mental health. Part of that process involved talking about me and my colleagues, and I didn't pull any punches in showing how many quirks and idiosyncrasies we have. Because I was connected with other, far more popular websites, my work reached a fairly large audience quickly. As feedback came in from readers, they more often than not commented on how surprised they were that shrinks had just as many problems—if not more— than their clients. They also seemed to like what some referred to as a "down-to-earth, honest, sometimes vulgar" approach to the material. As the site continued to grow with new readers, I decided that I would take my writing to another level and produce a book to show how all of us, both shrinks and patients alike, are what people call "crazy."

The day I started writing this book I was brimming with confidence. *This will be just like writing ShrinkTalk. Instead of it being one page, though, I'll just make it a few hundred. Maybe even a thousand! And it will have a great narrative arc and logical flow and be full of psychological insights and humor. But no cursing. Dad says that's undignified. I need to tone that down a bit.*

When I actually put my hands on the keyboard to write the world's greatest psychology book, however, my thought process suddenly changed. *Where to start? What is it I want to say? What is my goal again? I don't have one.*

"That's ridiculous," I said aloud, as if verbalizing my irrationality would trump my inner monologue. "Just do what you always do when you write: ramble incoherently about something related to psychology and pray that someone finds it remotely interesting."

My brain had other plans. *I have no clue what I want to write . . . I can't do this . . . I'll never be able to produce anything worthwhile . . . I'm going to fail . . .*

We saw with Bill that self-talk is powerful and can generate potent emotions. I could feel my heart rate increasing; it sensed that something was wrong. *Now I'm getting anxious. Why can't I just write the damn thing? What's wrong with me?*

Given actual danger—a tiger in the African jungle, a steroid-pumped bruiser ready to kill you for telling his girlfriend that "Shrinks do it for forty-five minutes an hour," or seeing Bill tearing down the highway toward you in his Mustang convertible—the body responds well, preparing for action. Adrenaline courses through you, and suddenly your fingernails are tingling and your breathing becomes shallow. Your shoulder blades tighten and sweat pours down from your forehead. The anxiety associated with staring down the barrel of a shotgun with an angry farmer at the end of it funnels through your veins.

The fight-or-flight mechanism had kicked in for me. Normally, there's some action to take to relieve this reaction. Run from the tiger. Hit the guy first. Shoot out Bill's tires. But sitting in my living room getting ready to type the first line of my book, there was no threat in front of me. Just a white screen, a blinking cursor, and my own brain now capable of not just depression but a panic attack as well. I was stuck in a feedback loop with nothing to flee from or fight. And yet my mind interpreted my physical reactions as signs that I was in danger. But what's the danger? Failure as a writer? My brain couldn't figure it out. So, unable to find the threat, it ratcheted up the adrenaline in case I couldn't argue the fact that I didn't mean shrinks do it for forty-five minutes with *his* girlfriend, just in general. The brain wanted to make sure I was ready to react even if it didn't know what it was responding to. I started typing a few words to distract myself, but I recognized that I needed to do more.

Remembering what to do when a panic attack sets in, I immediately dropped to the floor, faceup, and began doing what is known as diaphragmatic breathing. I essentially pushed my stomach out, taking in oxygen through my nose, not allowing my lungs to do the lame work they had been doing. *Count to four as I breathe in, SLOWLY, pushing the CO2 out through my mouth. Keep counting, keep breathing.* This allowed me to maximize the amount of oxygen being taken into my bloodstream. This helped my heart rate to slow down from what felt like 481,000 to a more-reasonable 140. And I continued to repeat the important facts about panic attacks: *It's a false alarm; I'm not going to die/faint/remain in this mode forever. In fact, if I kept my heart rate that high I'd pretty much just collapse from exhaustion.*

About three minutes later it was over. I stared up at the ceiling, noticing a crack in the molding I hadn't seen before, and wondering how, some ten-plus years after my first lecture on panic disorder, I had ended up having the first one of my entire life. The answer was actually quite simple: My mind and body had miscommunicated with each other.

I can't believe Pete goes through this on a daily basis.

When I got up from the floor I took stock of what I had created. I felt like I had emerged from a postapocalyptic war zone. In reality, it was a small pool of sweat on my chair, fingerprint smudges where I had grabbed the desk in terror, and seven words typed on the screen, three of which were "fuck."

Dad's not going to like this.

A few months after Pete's encounter with his incredibly well-endowed client and, by now, very sore girlfriend, I took Pete out for breakfast to try to understand more about his condition and its impact. It crossed my mind that since we were both on psychotropics now, alcohol might not be the best idea, but a pharmacist had told me that I should be all right on Zoloft so long as I wasn't funneling the booze, frat-boy style. The medicine was doing a decent job on my symptoms: no crying spells, lower anxiety, not waking up in the morning to two seconds of peace followed by the thought of "Oh right, I have to live today." All of that was gone. I still missed Janet, but she wasn't on my mind every single moment, and I had hope that time and therapy might take care of the rest.

Pete and I sat down in the corner of a small diner. It was basically empty, and yet Pete's eyes darted back and forth as we walked into the place, and he insisted on sitting with his back to the wall, quickly ordering a Bloody Mary.

"Is this *The Godfather*?" I asked. "Will someone stab you in the back if you're not paying attention?"

"You just don't get it, do you?" Pete said.

I didn't. "Pete, therapy for panic has a great track record, like 75 to 95 percent. I just completed successful therapy with a client who had panic disorder."

"Right. And what do you think happens to that 5 to 25 percent of people who don't improve?"

I paused, thinking that one day I might have to tell a client with panic that there was nothing I could do for him. "They are reduced to this?" I asked, looking him up and down with a sudden wave of empathy.

"You got it," he said. "Beta-blockers, Xanax, Klonopin, Ativan. I take pretty much everything my doctor will prescribe for me, plus the other stuff I don't tell anyone about."

"I just can't, for the life of me, figure out how you can success-fully treat someone for panic but not be able to help yourself."

"Cardiologists get heart problems, don't they?" asked Pete.

"It's not the same."

"But it is. If you have a problem with any organ in your body that isn't your brain, it's socially acceptable, and no one can blame you or ask you to do anything other than be a good patient. Take your drugs and let the doctors help you. Once it's up here, though," he said, tapping his index finger against his temple, "it's something that you should be able to *control*. Well, guess what? I can't. I can tell other people what to do and it usually works, but it doesn't translate to me."

"Can I ask what you do in your therapy?"

"At first," Pete said, "we did a lot of the standard stuff. My therapist and I reviewed diaphragmatic breathing to make sure I was doing it correctly."

In our graduate training I had learned how to do these breath-ing exercises to the point of mastery, having no idea that I'd need them myself more than ten years later.

"Then we started going through my self-talk. He didn't need to educate me on panic because I knew the score."

For some people, simply arming them with the knowledge of what panic attacks are (and aren't) can be helpful: *While extremely unpleasant they are not inherently dangerous. They won't cause you to faint or go crazy. And they will end for no other reason than the body will simply tire out.*

"What is your self-talk about?" I asked.

"I'm pretty classic, actually. I make the standard mistakes in my thinking. I predict the worst-case scenario and, of course, I tell myself that if it were to come true, it would be a complete disaster."

"You're not able to change that thinking?"

"When we're sitting here, after a few cocktails and my medica-tions are sliding around in my veins, sure. But when King Penis showed up and I was off my regimen, I immediately started to think, 'I'm doing something wrong by talking to him. He'll see I'm just a regular person and not some Super Therapist. Rob will see it too. They'll laugh at me and I'll never get over it.' I actually just made myself a little antsy from having said all that. Self-talk is fucking strong, you know that."

"But doesn't the fact that you are wrong time and time again change anything for you? No one thought you weren't Super Therapist. None of us laughed, at least not out loud. And even if we did, you didn't collapse."

"Actually," Pete said, "I kind of did."

"You know what I mean."

"I do. I hear you. And the answer is no, it doesn't change anything."

"What about PMR?" I asked. This stands for progressive muscle relaxation, which is based on the premise that when anxiety rises, muscle tension increases due to changes in blood flow. Clients with anxiety or panic are often taught how to relax their muscles through tightening and loosening every major group of muscles. When the muscles are more relaxed, anxiety decreases as a result of the lack of physiological arousal. This is more of a preventive technique when one senses an increase in nervousness, because once you're in the throes of full-blown panic, it's very difficult to simply relax your muscles.

"Again, it helps a bit but not all that much," Pete said, throwing back a second Bloody Mary.

"Does anything help? At all?"

"You know what helps, even more than this?" he said, holding up the empty glass. "Sticking my head in the freezer."

I had perhaps the world's smallest refrigerator in college, with a minute section of freezer that couldn't hold a quarter of my face. Picturing Pete shoving his head into that, having scratch marks on his cranium from the tiny stalactites and stalagmites in my dorm-room fridge, made me feel that much sorrier for him. And all the more curious about how many of my colleagues were coloring photos with gray crayons and shoving their faces into Frigidaires.

"How does it help?" I asked.

"The rush of the cold serves as a distraction. The ice on my face and neck, the freezing air going into my mouth and up my nostrils. It just reminds me of being in the Arctic or something, and I seem to feel a lot better. The sad thing is that you can't always find a freezer when you need one."

So distraction is what made Pete feel the best he could. Clients are rarely discouraged from using this as a therapeutic tool, but it doesn't address the problem directly. It's simply palliative; it keeps the swelling down.

I looked at Pete, who was ordering up his third Bloody Mary by this point. He knew how to do diaphragmatic breathing, he understood how to challenge self-talk, he was educated on what panic actually is, and he could complete exercises on muscle relaxation. That's treatment for panic in a nutshell, and yet Pete was in that small percentage of people who simply don't benefit.

"Pete, I'm really sorry that this is what it's like for you. For most clients all the rest of the stuff works. We've both had clients running in place, basically *inducing* a panic attack just so they can experience the feelings for what they are."

"Yep, and whenever I make them do that and they don't freak out, I think about how I can't even run a few city blocks without thinking I'm going to die. I fucking hate them for it." Another sip.

"What do you talk about in your therapy now? I mean, now that you don't have the 'cure'?"

"Coping, really," Pete said. "We talk about ways to minimize the symptoms, how to take the medications at the best times, and in the best combinations. You might think he's a bad therapist, but he's not. I feel accepted there, like even though I'm a head case, he doesn't judge me or make me feel bad about myself. He's supportive, even though we both know I might never kick this."

It's clients like Pete—those who achieve little therapeutic success—that can turn shrinks into burned-out shells of the young go-getters they once were.

"Do any of them know?" I asked.

"My clients?"

"Yeah."

"Of course not. And if they asked, there's no way I'm telling them. I can't have my credibility impaired."

Ten years later I still talk to Pete on a weekly basis for peer supervision/consultation. He knows that I write about him from time to time, and that's fine with him. He still uses every drug under the sun, but with minimal results. And although he is in that small group of people who suffer from an intractable case of panic disorder, he maintains a successful psychology practice. And of course none of his clients seem to think he has a single problem—that is, until they see him in a public forum. Then all bets are off.

11 a.m.
The Torture Chamber That Is OCD

Throughout my childhood I had three windows in my bedroom. When I was about twelve years old, each night before I went to sleep I had to open and close the shutters on each of them three times. Nine repetitions every night, without fail. If that did not happen, sleep would not come. Instead, I'd stare at the shutters, wide-eyed, tense. I'd ultimately get out of bed to finish the job. My mother, who for the longest time cherished the ground I walked on, would peer in with wonder. "He's doing research," she whispered to my stepfather, "studying the torque or gravity or something. He's going to be a rich engineer one day!"

At 10:30 a.m., Monday through Friday throughout high school, I had to smell my arms to see if I was "clean enough" since my morning shower. Even if I hadn't broken a sweat in PE and had simply sat in class, there I was, smelling myself. For four years I didn't question it or even attempt to curb the behavior, because I knew that without putting my nose to the skin near my elbow, an uncomfortable and agitated emotion would follow. My best friend wondered if there were times that I simply didn't "you know, feel so fresh," since I was so undeterred in my quest for olfactory satisfaction.

My mother always impressed upon me the importance of healthy skin. "If you're to be a successful lawyer someday, you'll want to look young and confident," she said. She then gave me a jar of Vaseline. "Rub this all over your face every night to keep wrinkles away." And from the ages of ten to nineteen, I did just that without a second thought, to the point that I developed an almost-permanent shine to my countenance. And if I ever did forget—a rare occurrence—an intense anxiety would take over as soon as I climbed into bed.

Hindsight is always 20/20, and I'd love to say that I wouldn't engage in that behavior again; however, despite what we want to believe, we sometimes hold onto messages from significant people throughout our lives. Thus, I keep a bottle of antiaging wrinkle cream next to my bed to this day. Strangely, I don't even use it in that location—only in the morning in the bathroom—but it simply needs to be there. If the dog walks off with it or it disappears under the bed, I become nervous. It's not a crippling anxiety, but something along the lines of *Something is wrong, something is . . . off. Maybe something bad will happen?*

Irrational? Of course. Emotionally palpable? Definitely. My eyes shift back and forth a bit like I'm pondering how to escape a crime scene. And when I finally do find the cream, the jitters disappear. The cream is a drug, and just seeing it gives me a fix. The world is right again.

My college roommate needed to be the sole person to touch the alarm before we went to sleep. We had bunk beds in our room, and I would climb up the small ladder into the loft-like space. I'd watch him gently set the alarm on the small cube that was our clock, slowly flick the switch to set the alarm, and then hold out his hands the way one would if the clock suddenly pulled out a gun. "It's okay, just take it easy," I'd picture him saying, as if the clock might change its mind and suddenly shut off. Or shoot him.

After my roommate backed away from what he saw as an overly temperamental wake-up device, he turned off the light, climbed into bed, pulled the covers over himself, and gave a sigh of relief, followed by "Good night, Rob." Almost mindlessly, I'd climb down

the ladder and walk over toward the desk where the clock sat. I'd
pretend to bump the desk with my hip or I'd grab a pencil near the
clock. "Oh, sorry, man," I'd say. "I might have hit the alarm clock.
I'll just reset it now." At eighteen years old I had no real concept of
obsessive-compulsive disorder and the ways it could manifest itself;
thus, what should have been empathy was actually enjoyment on
my end. An enjoyment I experienced nearly every night.

"No!" he'd yell and jump up out of bed, mumbling under his
breath how frustrating it was that he couldn't fall asleep without
pomp and circumstance for the ninety-second night in a row. "Just
get away from it and go to bed." Sometimes we'd repeat this ritual
multiple times on any given night until I finally got tired from all
the climbing to and from the bunk bed. I'd fall into a peaceful
sleep—my Vaseline tucked neatly under my arm—my roommate
lying just a few feet below me with bloodshot, rage-infested eyes.

Years later in graduate school, one of my professors, whom
I'll call Dr. Gail, left her faculty position to take on full-time private practice. "I'm no longer your superior, Rob," she said. "We're
friends now." Months later she invited me to lunch at her office.
Walking into her suite, I noticed a fairly large sign on the wall of
the waiting area: DO NOT MOVE THE CHAIRS IN THE WAITING ROOM!

Apparently some clients had been manipulating the chairs to
be able to put their feet up on the coffee table, causing Dr. Gail
some unnecessary anxiety. I'd always known that Gail was particular, but the capital letters in her admonishment suggested to me
that something more was at play here. Given that we were now
"friends," and remembering my cruel behavior toward my college
roommate, my first response was to attempt to turn one of the
chairs around, scurry to the office's kitchen area, and watch her
exasperated expression through a crack in the door. However, I
noticed a power drill and some thick bolts on the floor, then realized that she had actually bolted the chairs through the carpet and
into the concrete.

When I told Pete—who by this time was probably smoking a hefty amount of marijuana to calm his nerves around others—about Dr. Gail's unusual behavior, he regaled me with the rumors surrounding her idiosyncrasies. She had a cleaning woman come every day of the week to dust and disinfect, regardless of how dirty the office was, even on the weekends. She had a separate compartment for her food in the employee refrigerator, with a polite but firm note that said PLEASE DO NOT TOUCH ANYTHING IN THIS DRAWER. No one had even seen her shake hands with clients, and on a day that a colleague of hers had run thirty city blocks to get to the office in the sweltering heat because she couldn't catch a cab, and asked her for a sip from her water bottle, she refused. When her office partner confronted her with, "Damn, Gail, you are really OCD sometimes," she replied, "No, no—that's a serious mental illness. I'm just quirky."

Quirky. That made sense. Although the DSM-IV generally (and erroneously) diagnoses in a categorical fashion (i.e., you either have a condition or you don't; there are rarely *degrees* of mental illness), OCD would clearly be the exception. Was I, Gail, or my old roommate actually *impaired?* Not exactly. We weren't in treatment for it; we still lived our lives, just with certain demands. So maybe it was more of a mild neurotic reaction that many people share. In fact, I once spoke to a man at a party who told me he had been diagnosed with OCD, yet didn't seem all that incapacitated by it. "Alex" described himself as a chronic masturbator, someone who had spent years perfecting a schedule to allow him dozens of opportunities to pleasure himself on a daily basis. He told his coworkers he suffered from irritable bowel syndrome so that he could excuse himself to use the restroom an unusual number of times per day. He bought a train set that he put in his basement so his housemates thought he had a more-traditional hobby. He was so focused on pleasuring himself that he even bought special masturbation gloves. They came in six different colors, with varying textures, designed for the "man who knows how to love himself the best." Apparently these gloves were to promote "safe self sex" (whatever *that* means). And Alex didn't describe significant distress at all; in fact, he was fairly proud of the way he managed his life. This wasn't due to lack of insight; he recognized the inherent "left of center" in his lifestyle, but just like Gail, he too saw himself as simply quirky.

After six years of graduate study, noting how interesting all of us were with our aberrations, I started to believe true OCD didn't exist. At least, not in the way textbooks and documentaries described it, where people's lives were completely overrun by it. In fact, I had spent more time drawing pictures of Janet and me making out on the beach as I threw back beer and Zoloft than these so-called OCD victims used to wash their hands for fear of contamination. But then I met a man I'll call David, and I gained a new perspective on the disorder.

David came to therapy with me regularly for about one year. However, simply getting to his appointments was agonizing for him; it got so bad that I considered making house calls to get him started. David couldn't leave the house, not even to run a quick errand, without first going through a ritual that included opening and closing every drawer in every room at least twice, locking each window in the home—even though he lived on the twentieth floor of a high-rise—and checking the stove multiple times to make sure he had shut it off. He hadn't been able to hold down a high-paying position despite his MBA from a prestigious university, and his persistent tardiness due to his compulsive behavior put him in continual danger of losing his part-time job as an office worker.

When David would finally arrive at work, he arranged his chair so he could sit at a perfect 90-degree angle in line with the office wall clock. He refused to write with anything but a blue-ink pen. If he was handed a different type of pen, or worse, a pencil, he approached literal paralysis. He just sat there, staring, his writing hand hovering over the legal pad, frozen.

When he returned home, David shaved his head with a straight razor, and then checked with a mirror to make sure there wasn't a single hair left on his scalp. If he failed to perform any one of these tasks, David experienced a crippling and intense anxiety. I asked him on many occasions to tell me what the feeling was like, and every time the answer was the same: "Rob, let me handcuff you with your hands behind your back, then stuff you into a straitjacket. We'll go up to the top of the Empire State Building and I'll dangle you over the edge as I hold you up with just one pinkie along the chain of the cuffs. If you can imagine the anxiety that comes with that, you're about 10 percent of the way toward understanding what I feel."

According to the DSM-IV, true OCD afflicts 2 percent of all Americans. If the disorder is severe, it is extremely difficult to treat, with many clients needing to be placed into inpatient settings to get round-the-clock care. Many believe that the disorder is biologically based, which is why many practitioners understandably push for medication to treat the condition. David was by far the most severe case I had ever heard of, let alone seen. At age twenty-six he had managed to maintain his rudimentary functioning through a very large dose of Luvox. His doctor and family, however, had urged him to seek therapy as well. Broadly speaking, therapy combined with medication has a greater success rate than either treatment alone, so this was good advice. But when we discussed prognosis, I was obligated to tell him the facts: At best, he could hope for about a 70 percent remission of symptoms, assuming he remained in treatment and continued his medication.

What made David such an interesting person was that while some of his obsessions were based on fears that had at least a grain of wisdom (e.g., "If I don't check the stove, it is *technically possible* that a fire could start while I'm away"), others carried no rationality whatsoever ("If I use a pencil, then something—I don't know what, exactly, but rest assured, it will be awful—will happen"). David recognized this incongruity, but even thoughts that were completely lacking in empirical evidence drove him to the point of hysteria; they *felt* so true that they must be, in fact, accurate. This is known as emotional reasoning.

Over the years, psychologists and psychiatrists have developed a treatment for OCD called exposure/response prevention (EX/RP), a system we fancy to be so complex that entire journals and conferences have been devoted to its study. Sadly, this approach is, in many ways, a torture chamber for most clients—not because of the intricacies of the treatment, but because of the sheer agony of its simplicity. Boiled down to its essentials, the client has to stop the compulsions, plain and simple. Be it counting, washing, checking, or any of the dozens of maladaptive coping behaviors available, he has to simply stop doing it, no matter how much it hurts. He has to sit with the pain, experience it, tolerate it. The idea is to let your anxiety peak until it ultimately diminishes. In some rudimentary ways it's similar to drug withdrawal: You yearn for that fix; it consumes you as the sweat and tears pour down your face. The drug calls to you and you sit still, not giving in. Then, after enough time, you start to experience habituation, a lack of need for the drug.

In David's case, an example would be to look in the mirror after work (exposure) and simply refuse, come hell or high water, to take out that razor and remove any stubs of hair. The theory states that the resultant anxiety is essentially a false alarm—an erroneous belief that danger is present, that something horrible will happen. With repeated practice at doing nothing, the body and mind will realize that there is no inherent catastrophe waiting to happen. When this occurs, the anxiety will decrease and the need to engage in the compulsions will diminish.

The therapist has several tasks to perform with this treatment. The first and most important is to sell the EX/RP model. When I told David what we would be doing to help him, he understandably balked. "If I understand this correctly," he said, "you'd like me to actually attempt to *not* fight off my anxiety and *not* do any of the things I need to do to feel better. I'm paying you to do nothing?"

Sadly, yes. "I know, it sounds ridiculously simplistic and perhaps counterintuitive, but this is how it works: Your mind has tricked you into thinking that if you sit at an angle other than 90 degrees, something horrible will happen. You can't just tell yourself 'That's not true'; you can't rationalize it out. You have to experience it; you have to show yourself, demonstrate to your mind and body, that it's simply not the case."

"OCD is a mindfuck? Is that what you're saying?"

"Exactly. The pills you are taking help somewhat, but I need you to do this if we are to have any hope of making a more-significant dent in your symptoms. You're hooked on razors, blue pens, and checking your home. It's your cocaine. We need to wean you off of that."

It feels almost sadistic to ask a client to engage in such psychologically brutal behaviors knowing full well that the treatment will have clear limits. And yet that's what therapists do with severe OCD clients on a daily basis.

We created a hierarchy of the compulsions to be addressed. Some clients have behaviors over which they have at least some level of control, and those are tackled first. This provides not only a chance to learn coping skills during more painful compulsions but also increases the likelihood of success at the onset of treatment, which can serve as a motivating force. Unfortunately, David viewed every compulsion as equally crippling, and any hierarchy we developed had a significant level of arbitration to it.

My second responsibility was to demonstrate relaxation techniques and cognitive exercises to help to reduce the anxiety. Because this treatment is torturous, the client must have a psychological toolbox available to help him cope with the intense feelings. He needs a skill set that may include breathing exercises, muscle relaxation, visual imagery, distraction—the same tools often used in the treatment of panic. All of these can serve some palliative purpose.

Every week, David and I spent forty-five minutes, sometimes more, going through drills. We'd use what are known as subjective units of distress (SUDS), which served as a rough gauge of his levels of anxiety. I'd make him write with a black pen and order him to stare at his hair growth in a mirror while sitting at different angles from the clock. He'd give me an SUD at the beginning of the exercise, using a scale of 1 to 10. His initial reaction would often be "19!," but after a minute or so he'd settle into the formula we'd agreed upon.

I'd teach him to breathe from his diaphragm instead of his lungs. Because of the increased oxygen to his heart, he took in air more efficiently and felt a physiological relief. That might move him from a 10 to a 9. I taught him how to relax his muscles using focusing techniques. "Slowly roll your shoulders. Feel the muscle fibers loosening a bit. You might feel some tingling in your shoulder blades. That's okay, enjoy that feeling. Just picture your muscles settling down, relaxing." That might get him to an 8. If he pictured his mother cheering him on, he could get to a 7. For homework he would do the same thing in his apartment multiple times per day, attempting to teach his brain that nothing horrible would happen if he didn't follow his routines. It drained him, and it pained me to push him. I felt as if I was asking an alcoholic to sit in a bar all day and drink Pepsi. And, similar to alcoholism, relapse is very common when OCD is so severe.

My third responsibility was to provide motivation, to cheerlead. This was very difficult when I knew the statistics of recovery and recognized that the deck was so stacked against David. Yes, David could have been "one of the lucky ones," and somehow become symptom-free, but we both recognized how unlikely this would be. That said, because it's far too easy for clients to fall back into their old habits, to have that relief wash over them when they check the stove to make sure it's still off, I needed to continue to push David for something more than that so he didn't run out of psychological gas. Moving from an arbitrary figure of 10 to 7 might be a lot for some, very little for others.

For David it meant everything from a psychological-achievement perspective, but little in terms of his daily functioning. He was still late for work, got little accomplished, and had cuts on his head from the razor. He could use the black pen for five minutes but ultimately needed the blue. He could avoid shaving his scalp for an hour after his return from work, sometimes even for a whole day, but then he was back at it. His chair could be at an unusual angle for part of the morning but ultimately needed to go back into position. It was only when he finally engaged in the compulsion that the anxiety truly evaporated, only to return minutes later when he realized that he might have missed a hair or that the office seat might be just slightly off. That's a hallmark of OCD's nefariousness: tolerance. You get the relief but, ironically, the calm that washes over you perpetuates the very behavior that generated the faux relief you initially sought. It's a vicious cycle.

Ultimately, David got fired from his job. At that point we agreed that he needed a greater level of care. I couldn't give him any more than I had. David went to an inpatient unit and ultimately needed to be in what is known as a partial hospitalization program, where he spent the majority of his day in treatment. Months later, he called me.

"Hi, David," I said. "Where are you?"

"I'm at the hospital. I'm working on my OCD."

"I'm really glad to hear that. How is it going for you?"

"Eh, I can't say great. My brain is fucked up, you know?"

"I hear you. But you'll keep working the program?"

"Of course. I'm not a quitter, but I also know to keep my expectations real. Rob?"

"Yes?"

"Thank you for trying. I've read a lot of books on this, and you did what you're supposed to do. I'll never be normal, whatever that is, but thank you for trying."

"David, anyone in my position would have done the same thing."

"I don't care about anyone else. I met *you*, and thank *you* for trying. You know?"

"Yes. And you're welcome. David? I'm sorry. I wish I could have done more for you."

"I know, Rob. Maybe I'll see you on the 'outside,' huh?"

"I hope so. My door will always be open for you."

I thought about my roommate and how I had tortured him. I thought about Gail and the chairs bolted to the floor. I cursed out my mother for making me fear the sun, that giant ball of flames that causes wrinkles. We had all suffered in our own way, but this was nothing compared to David's plight. He was truly debilitated and, unless he was one of the few, very lucky people who had some sort of spontaneous remission, a "cure" of any sort was highly unlikely.

For months I wondered if I had failed him. Did I deliver the treatment in the appropriate way? Did I motivate him enough? Should I have pushed inpatient treatment sooner? None of those questions encapsulated what went wrong, and David certainly didn't see it that way. And yet I took his time, energy, and money, in exchange for what? A service that he ultimately couldn't use? No one should be given a guarantee when they walk through the door, because predicting therapy outcome is not easy due to the eccentric nature of the human condition. And no healing professions work on contingency; your doctor gets paid whether he or she "cures" you or not. And yet there's a certain guilt in accepting a check at the end of each session where you and the client have an unspoken message: Well, we're trying our best.

Could it be that I didn't fail—rather, that David failed himself? No, that wasn't right either. He worked hard, harder than anyone I had ever seen. He thought he could beat it. He battled. But it was as if he was running with a shattered leg. There was something broken within him. It wasn't his fault.

The truth about David's problem was that the disease can at times be too strong for medicine, therapy, or both, or any other concoctions that can be labeled as therapeutic. Severe OCD lays bare the fact that mental health treatment has its limitations, a ceiling effect, a breakdown of sorts with problems and disorders that are simply intractable. What makes this more sobering is the fact that this might not ever change. Unless we develop new insights or state-of-the-art medications, practitioners like me will not only be neurotic with our facial creams and chairs bolted to the floor, but also yearning for something else to help our patients who are struggling with a pain that is destroying their lives.

12 p.m.
No One Else Can See or Hear It, Yet It's Still There

The term *psychosis* has received numerous definitions over the years; unfortunately, none of them has been universally accepted by the field. For the average person, however, psychosis equals craziness. Many of us imagine that people who suffer from psychotic disorders are the ones sitting in the white, padded rooms in hospitals or begging for change on city streets while screaming at a person no one else can see. Professionals often diagnose them with schizophrenia or perhaps delusional disorder, but in the public's eyes they are just "fucked up": They smell bad, they're extremely violent, and they are to be avoided at all costs.

I think most of us in graduate school fancied ourselves in a different camp than the rest of society, but the reality was that few were jumping at the chance to work with those diagnosed with such severe illnesses as schizophrenia. At twenty-four, I was afraid. Not of being attacked, mind you, but more because of that general anxiety that comes from potentially awkward conversations. *What if he doesn't answer my questions? What if he thinks I'm trying to read his thoughts? What if he simply talks to the wall?*

To help us to understand more about psychosis, our professors gave us a soundtrack that was designed to simulate the experience of auditory hallucinations. The tape was created in part by people who were in treatment for schizophrenia, and we were asked to conduct our day-to-day business for as long as possible while listening to the soundtrack on headphones.

What I heard was multiple, sometimes incoherent voices switching from ear to ear in a never-ending pattern. *Grrrrr, you suck, fuckin', fuckin', hate you, HATE YOU!! You, you, you loser! Coward. Grrrr.* Over and over, deep male voices paired with shrill female wailing. *They're looking at you, they know you're a fraud, they will all get you . . .*

I went to the library, the student center, and a local restaurant while wearing the headphones. When I tried to order anything that contained more than one ingredient I was looked at askance by the waitress. I had to close my eyes to drown out the sounds and coalesce my thoughts. *I'd like a cheeseburger. With . . . lettuce and onions and . . .* Then I'd open my eyes to reorient myself, only to snap them closed again . . . *Ketchup.* I couldn't speak if I needed to look at whoever was listening to me.

"Okay," the waitress said, looking over her shoulder, probably for backup in case I brandished a shotgun. "Do you want fries with that?"

"Yes!" I'd say as quickly as possible, giving it no thought.

"Well, we have regular, Cajun, sweet potato, cheese, double cheese, or sweet potato Cajun cheese."

Simply absorbing the choices was nearly impossible, let alone picking one. I ultimately decided to go with the simplest answer at all times—*The first one, please*—even if that meant dying from a food allergy.

When I got home and took off the headphones, an uncontrollable pity came over me. It went far beyond the simple "Wow, that sounds really hard" approach, to a greater, very painful attempt at understanding the plight of those with active psychosis. It made sense: How could these people hold a job if they can't organize their thoughts? While many psychotics seem flat and depressed on the outside, they are actually roiling within. How do you *not* eventually answer a voice that speaks to you, that plays in your head over and over, even if no one else can hear it? And, worse, the fact that I knew the field doesn't have a single, coherent reason *why* this even occurs in people made it all the more frustrating.

Despite popular belief, most people suffering from psychosis are not violent. In fact, those diagnosed with schizophrenia only have a slight increase in likelihood for violence compared to the general population. However, it is over four times more likely when substance abuse is involved. And although the DSM-IV is filled with obscure diagnoses and conditions that most clinicians will never see, the relatively uncommon case of schizophrenia combined with violent behavior came to me somewhat early in my career.

In graduate school I was assigned to a psychiatric emergency room as an intake worker. The job generally consisted of meeting with suicidal or actively mentally ill patients and making diagnoses or treatment decisions. More often than not, the patients were admitted for treatment in one of the inpatient wards until they were "mentally stable," at which time they were released to a less-restrictive level of care.

My office was a seven-by-eleven-foot space with bare white walls, save for a portrait of the hospital president staring down at me. When I arrived at work that day, the nursing assistant advised me that there was a new patient in my office who had come to the hospital of his own volition because of "acute depression." "No orderlies necessary," she told me. "Your supervisor is down the hall if you need him." With a coffee in one hand and attaché case in the other, I made a critical error as soon as I entered the room. As a precaution that is unnecessary 99.9 percent of the time, a clinician often sits between the patient and the door. This allows for a simple means of egress should the patient demonstrate any potential signs of violence.

What I was thinking that day, at that time, is something that escapes me now. I walked into my office, past the man seated immediately to my right, and plopped down at the far end of the room. As soon as my butt hit the cushion I noticed that the man was big. Not colossal, professional-wrestler big, but certainly large enough to easily do significant damage to me. A patient's size in and of itself is no cause for alarm, so I simply spoke calmly. "Hello, I'm Rob Dobrenski. I'm the intake worker here. I'll be taking down some basic information and asking you some questions about why you're here. This will help me and my supervisor decide how best to help you."

The man, who was probably in his early forties, seemed agreeable enough with my initial statements, but irritable nonetheless. "Are you going to give me medication?" he asked.

"I'm not a physician, so I won't be doing that personally, but it's possible one of the doctors will want to give you something. Do you take anything now?"

"No, and that's by choice. I've been on things before and they've screwed me up."

"What have you taken?"

"Lots of stuff."

"Can you remember any names? That would help a lot."

"No, but I can tell you that if you give me Haldol, I'll fuck you up."

I had very little knowledge about medications then, and didn't know that Haldol is an antipsychotic.

"What happens if you take Haldol?" I asked.

"IF YOU GIVE ME HALDOL, I'LL FUCK YOU UP!" he yelled as he leaned forward.

When patients are excessively loud or aggressive without provocation, it is important to understand the underpinnings of their behavior. However, a firm stance is necessary to ensure that fear and intimidation are not part of the relationship.

"Let's back up a second," I said. "I was told that you are here because you're depressed. I'd like to find out more about that. But I must insist that you lower your voice and calm down. I'm only trying to help you."

He stood up. "How old are you?"

Without thinking I said, "I'm twenty-seven."

"You're just a fucking kid," he said in an angry tone.

I started graduate school when I was twenty-four years old and was laughed at by most of the adult clients I saw. My baby face—probably still shiny from all of the Vaseline absorbed years earlier—put me more in the fourteen- to seventeen-year-old range, and that scared people. They were never really worried about my age per se; they had come to talk about painful things, and that was scary. They wondered whether someone who looked so young could possibly help them. In a way, this might have been considered a test: Would I react with confidence and empathy, or would I get defensive? My response would give the client a preview of how I would respond when they began to talk about what was troubling them. Would I step up and help, or crash and burn in a fire of youth and naiveté?

For the most part I did well at letting clients express that fear without getting on my haunches in a bout of defensiveness. However, remembering days of embarrassment after being laughed out of bars for looking so young by people who looked a lot like the man in front of me, my emotions sometimes got the best of me. Sometimes I would counter this by using a therapeutic approach often called "As If." If you want to be a confident person, act "as if" you are that person. Don't wait to *feel* confident. In short, play the role and your emotions will follow suit.

And so I responded, "I don't think twenty-seven is a kid. And I know what I'm doing, so maybe you should just answer my questions and keep the commentary to yourself."

The man's eyes narrowed to slits. "You a wise guy, kid? You know I've killed someone before?"

Ironically, it was in fact my youth and naiveté that was creating this growing problem. It was a huge mistake to be smug and over-confident, but that's just what I was doing. "Oh? Is that a fact?" I said, not buying his proclamation.

"Yes, so don't screw with me."

"Who did you kill? Someone young and naive like me?"

At that point he started to walk toward me, and that's when I realized my arrogance would prove to be my downfall. Anxiety lurched from the bottom of my stomach to the top of my throat. The only other furniture in the room was a desk that sat between the two chairs we occupied, under which was a small panic button. I reached forward. My hand hit the button just as he reached for my neck. Fortunately, my staff nametag was attached to a break-able necklace that gave way as he pulled on it, and I was able to squirm away and scurry over the desk in terror.

By the time the man turned around I was behind him, opening the door. The orderlies appeared in the doorway and I sprinted past them, down the hall, past the nurses' station, and out into the parking lot, where I stood panting, bent over, my hands on my knees. One of the nurses came out and asked me what happened. I told her the story and emphasized, almost in tears, how it was basically my fault, that I had provoked him. She told me that the orderlies had restrained the man and she sent me home. Days later I found out that the man suffered not from depression, but from paranoid schizophrenia and substance dependence, and had active hallucinations that people were trying to poison him with antipsychotic medication.

On the night I was sent home I sat in a rocking chair for hours, trying to process the experience. I did the same thing for a few nights after that. "You are so stupid, so cocky—it's your fault." I didn't sound all that different from the voices on the tape I had listened to years before. I met with my supervisor in his office weeks after the event and he asked me how I was feeling.

"I've been better."

He stubbed out a cigarette. "Rob, you're going to have to understand that what we do isn't an exact science. As a field we don't know all that much about schizophrenia or the related conditions. We're all pretty new at this."

"I do understand that."

"No, you don't. If you understood that, you'd know that because of the very nature of our work and the fly-by-the-seat-of-our-pants approach we all take at times, mistakes will be made. You thought that by challenging him he would respect you, or at least not be aggressive. It backfired. It happens. You've learned something from this. If you don't give yourself room to screw up, you'll never really grow."

I tried to take what he had said to heart, to forgive myself for provoking the man, putting myself in danger, and, most importantly, for not giving the man what he needed at the time. He deserved a more empathic ear and less cockiness. For months after that I was unusually cautious with people who had psychosis, gingerly working my way back to a level of comfort.

Since that day, I've never had another encounter with violence in my practice. The increased self-awareness and minimization of my hubris made the work much more enjoyable, and these traits served me well with other psychotic patients. Although that initial experience could have been significantly worse, I clearly learned my lesson the hard way.

During the early days of my private practice, I met a man I'll call Jim. It was difficult to believe this middle-aged man in khakis and a neat button-down shirt when he confessed that he was delusional, perceiving that his coworkers were out to get him. "I can't shake the anxiety that goes with it, and there's a part of me that believes it's not true, but deep down I know I have delusional disorder."

"How do you know that?" I asked.

"I know. I'm a psychiatrist."

Psychiatrists are generally considered the top of the mental health food chain. They are physicians; they prescribe the psychotropic medications that so many people need. While they don't have as much formal training in psychology per se as psychologists, very few would argue that the term *doctor* is more typically associated with medical professionals—MDs—than those with a PhD. Therefore, they tend to get the most respect. This fact made the situation all the more unusual. A psychotic doctor? Like Pete said, cardiologists get heart problems, so is it that unreasonable to assume that a psychiatrist could have, perhaps, a chemical imbalance or even a structural abnormality in his brain? What if his patients knew? He would be ruined.

Treatment with other professionals has some distinct advantages. Most are familiar with the various therapeutic approaches. They generally know what to anticipate from you and what is expected of them in treatment. They usually respect your time and can appreciate the importance of being punctual and working hard to get the best results. Most have also worked with people who either did not or could not successfully work within a therapeutic framework and know how hard the job can be at times. They usually "get it," and are therefore very good clients.

"What medication are you taking?" I asked him.

"That's the thing," he said. "I want to do this without medicine."

It's no secret that mental health medications remain taboo for many people. No one walks into a pharmacy full of shame when he hands over a prescription for something to control his migraines. But some of us have a nagging fear that when we give the pharmacist the script for an antidepressant, he might yell out,

"What does this script say? Prozac?" So I understood where Jim was coming from in certain ways. But a physician who is against medication for a psychotic condition? This was almost unheard of.

"Jim, you're a doctor. You know that there's basically no data to support the treatment of an active psychosis without medication."

"I want to try without it," he said.

"Why?"

"Meds mean that I'm like . . . you know . . . sick. Crazy."

I felt anger well up in me, an urge to defend the people who put themselves out and say, *I can't do this alone. I need help.* "Is that what you tell your patients, *Doctor?* 'You're crazy'?"

"No, no, no, of course not. And I don't really think they are. There's just a feeling . . . a wrong feeling about *me* taking it."

Many people have very tolerant views about other people taking psychotropic drugs, but the rules don't always apply to themselves. Because deep down, in the nether regions of their psyches, they still see having a mental disorder as a weakness.

"We spend our lives trying to debunk these myths," I said. "That therapy, medication, and anything else we do to help isn't about being crazy or weak. Yet you think that about yourself." Confronting Jim like this had risks. We hadn't known each other more than thirty minutes, so there was little to no foundation of a working relationship. He also suffered from delusions that could have easily been triggered by what I was saying. *You're just like them—out to get me.* But clearly my own anger at his shortsightedness had an impact on my judgment.

"No," I said.

"What do you mean, no?"

"I mean that I won't work this way. Maybe you can find someone who will, but I don't believe someone like yourself, in this state, who has been battling delusions for God knows how long with no results, can get significant relief without medicine. I can't show you a perfect research study, but I'm sure we both agree there's a biological basis for what you have. That would be best served with medicine. I wouldn't be giving you proper help if I ignored that premise. If you want to work with me, you'll need to consult with one of your peers about medication, and then you and I will need to address your feelings about it."

Our appointment concluded with Jim saying, "I'll think about it." I didn't hear from him for another five weeks, and he didn't return two phone calls from me to inquire about his well-being.

Eventually he contacted me and arranged for a second appointment. He was taking Zyprexa, a common antipsychotic. Grudgingly.

"Jim, I'm very glad that you've come back. I was concerned that I got a bit aggressive with you and scared you off."

"No, it's not that. I just needed time to really think about the medication issue."

"How do you feel with the medication?"

"Honestly? Better," he said. "I'm not delusional anymore, at least not by DSM standards. I've still got some anxieties, but the meds are doing their job. I just hate what it means."

"What does it mean?"

"It means I'm weak."

Like Bill, Jim was ready to hear more about how his thoughts were impeding his progress.

"Okay, this is good. You're familiar with how cognitive therapy works. It's about treating our thoughts as hypotheses. Those are testable. You have a theory that you are weak, but I need you to tell me how you drew that conclusion, other than by simply taking Zyprexa."

"I'm not sure how I could prove that."

"Let's try this, then," I said. "Could you give me the character-istics of a weak person?"

"Just a generic 'weak' person?"

"Yes."

"I suppose that would be someone who has no self-control whatsoever. Gives in to every whim. Can't rein in any impulses. Doesn't stick up for himself at all. Has no discipline."

"Okay, good. Now, if I remember correctly, you have a wife and kids. What would they say about you as a person?"

"A few weeks ago they'd have said I'm fucking crazy for thinking that my peers wanted to see me fired from the hospital."

"And you were off-base about that idea, right?"

"Yes."

"What would they say about you, as a person, now?"

"That I'm a pretty good husband and dad."

"Are you a *responsible* husband and father?"

"Of course."

"How so?" I said. "Tell me how you're responsible."

"I'm a good partner. My wife and I decide on family rules together. I provide financial stability to the home. My kids are happy but have rules and respect boundaries. I come home at night; I'm not an addict; I don't betray my wife."

"But you could, right? You're a good-looking doctor, you have a good income. You could probably get your share of extramarital activity, no?"

Jim chuckled at this. "I don't know about 'my share,' but yes, I could be a little freer if I chose to."

"But you choose not to."

"Right. I love my wife. I can resist those things."

"You see where I'm going with this?" I said.

"Yes, of course. It makes sense, kind of."

"You don't sound convinced."

"It's just that it makes sense rationally, but . . . it's just that. It makes sense rationally."

This is a common phenomenon in therapy. People tend to recognize healthy ways of looking at things, but only at an intellectual level. It's not part of them yet; it's not visceral. It needs to be more fully absorbed.

"It's like you believe it in your head, but maybe not your heart?" I asked.

"Yeah, it's just cerebral right now."

"That makes perfect sense to me. You've probably gotten in some good practice around this 'I'm weak' idea. It's going to take some time to unravel that ball of deception to get the new belief in place."

"What is the new belief?"

"I have an idea of what *I'd* like you to believe about medication, but why don't you take a stab at it first."

He paused. "I'm just thinking about what I'd tell my patients . . ."

"Go ahead—go with that."

"It just means that I have an illness. I'm sick. I have delusional disorder. It's probably biological."

"Nothing more, nothing less," I said. "Can you be okay with that?"

"I suppose I have to be," he said, but not in a fully resigned way.

Jim spent weeks challenging this notion of being "weak" because he needed to be on Zyprexa. Over time he softened his stance and treated himself less harshly. He accepted the fact that he had an illness. And the Zyprexa did an outstanding job of controlling the delusions around work. Because of this, his personal psychiatrist highly advised against him coming off it.

Like Pete, to this day Jim doesn't share his illness with his patients. He decided that his career would never sustain the inevitable backlash from patients who trust him to provide comprehensive psychiatry. The public has limits on what it will allow from those in the health professions. If a surgeon gets treatment for an alcohol problem and remains sober, will his patients automatically trust him again? Fortunately, Jim never jeopardized a patient's care because of his illness, as he immediately suspended his practice when his symptoms first emerged. Thus, he decided to maintain his right to privacy after he began seeing clients again. However, he does consult with his peers on a regular basis to ensure that he is doing his job at full capacity.

Jim will likely be on medication for the rest of his life. Talk therapy, especially the "tough love" aspect of our work, helped him to put his problems into a healthier perspective and decide what to do about his career. He is now in significantly greater control of his thought processes, which is what he originally sought out. The combination of medication and therapy put him in a better place. Jim isn't the norm, however. Unfortunately, many patients who suffer from psychosis don't get his results.

For almost one year, I wore sunglasses during every session with a woman whom I'll call Elaine. Elaine was a woman in her early sixties who had been diagnosed with schizoaffective disorder forty years prior. This is, in overly simple terms, a condition where both the symptoms of schizophrenia as well as a mood disorder (such as major depression) are present in a person's life. She had spent months at a time in the local psychiatric hospital for her inability to function because of her symptoms, which sometimes included feeling suicidal. When she left the hospital after her most recent stay and was given my card, her referring psychiatrist called me to let me know that if I wasn't wearing sunglasses upon her arrival, the session would never happen.

In my office at that time there was one twenty-watt bulb in a small lamp on the far end of the room, near the therapy couch, about twenty feet from where I sat. In the summer it wasn't a big deal, because the sunlight came in through the closed drapes well into the evening. But in wintertime, when it got darker at such an early hour, it was nearly impossible to see anything. Elaine liked it that way. Actually, she insisted, believing that with enough light my higher cortical powers would allow me to shoot hurtful thoughts through my glasses, across the room, through *her* dark sunglasses, and into her frontal lobe. That was her fear, which had gone on for years, and no medication or therapy had changed that. She was known at her local drugstore as the "bulb and glasses lady" because of the sheer amount she purchased of those two items.

Psychosis almost always equates with an inability to view the world rationally. You can tell those who suffer from bizarre delusions that what they believe makes no sense. You can present them with evidence to the contrary. But for whatever reason, be it a chemical imbalance, an alteration in brain structure, poor mothering, or some combination of the dozens of theories for psychosis, these people are simply unable to restructure their thoughts when it comes to their view of the world. For Elaine, the glasses meant protection, from me and most other people in the world. And yet she agreed that our goal for treatment should be to eliminate her primary delusion: that people could use their minds to damage her. She knew that medication was required but, unlike Jim, hers was not helping her significantly.

With Elaine I tried every therapeutic technique in my arsenal. I gave her strong doses of empathy, which had been helpful for Scott as he worked through his issues with obesity and fatherhood. I attempted to modify her thoughts like I did with Bill, as he grappled with his loss of sight. I asked her to show me how people penetrated her brain, to demonstrate how it worked, hoping in vain that her lack of logic might jar something in her rational mind. We discussed her past in depth, looking to uncover links between lessons she had learned as a child and present-day paranoia. No results.

Because Elaine hadn't made any progress over many months I had an ethical dilemma. Although she was dedicated to the treatment, nothing was working, and because of that I had a responsibility to discontinue treatment if I believed there was no possibility of change. Before we got to that point, however, I decided that I would make one attempt to *show* her that nothing would happen if we were bare-eyed together, rather than simply attempt to prove her ideas wrong through logic and debate.

"Elaine, we are running out of options for your treatment. I hate to say this, but I'm not hopeful."

This scared her. "Are you going to kick me out of treatment?"

"I'm saying that I'd like us to try, just for a little while, sitting here with our glasses off. I don't know of anything else that might be useful."

This is sometimes known as flooding, a technique traditionally used in treating phobias. It is based on the concept that when a client is presented with her irrational fear at full capacity—in this case, having our sunglasses off—that her anxiety will initially spike. But as her body and mind recognize there is no danger, the anxiety will ultimately diminish (a process known as extinguishing, as seen in the treatment of OCD). This, however, is a risky idea when dealing with people who are psychotic. The trauma of the event could trigger thoughts of suicide or a regression into further delusions.

"I can't do that," she said definitively.

"Okay, I understand. You're afraid. And I'm not going to lie, it will be very scary. But it might help. We've exhausted almost all other treatment methods, and we need to try this if we want to keep working together."

"And what if it fails?"

"If it fails, then I'd like us to consider more-intensive treatment—a day program or a partial hospitalization program."

"I don't want that," she said.

"I don't either, but if I can't give you what you need, then we have to go with other options. Let's try this and see what happens."

"Just . . . just for a second."

Elaine's hands shook as she lifted them from her lap. To her credit, she got her hand up to her face and got the glasses off, revealing what were surprisingly beautiful green eyes. I slowly took off my glasses as she finished.

"Elaine, is this okay? How do you feel?"

"I'm scared. You could hurt me."

"I won't hurt you, I promise. Just sit for a minute with me and let's see how you feel."

"This is dangerous."

"It is not dangerous, not at all. Try to just sit with the fear and let's see where things go."

She stared at me with a combination of suspicion and terror. I smiled as best I could, giving her a warm look, a cheerleader's expression. *You can do this; hang in there.*

She couldn't, however. The glasses went back on and she insisted I put mine on too. When I initially refused, she got up to leave the session. I put them back on.

"I'm sorry, Rob. I can't do this."

"Please don't apologize. It's your illness that causes this, not you."

"It's not going to get any easier, is it?"

"I don't think so, Elaine. At least not with me. You need more than this. You need daily work; you need to be with doctors who can try new medicines and work on creating the right combination of pills for you. You need intensive therapy, multiple times per week, so that you get plenty of practice at interacting with people without glasses. We can certainly keep trying, but this problem is so engrained that I'd be lying to you if I thought the outcome would be positive. I'm sorry, Elaine."

Elaine insisted on trying the techniques many more times, and some could argue that this, in and of itself, was progress. I agreed to try for a few more weeks, but unfortunately, no results were seen. At one point Elaine needed to be hospitalized again for suicidal thoughts, and all of us who had worked with her over the years agreed that she needed to be in a more-structured program with greater intensity, most likely on a permanent basis.

Treatment failure with Elaine reminded me of David, the OCD sufferer. Who was at fault: Elaine, me, therapy, the medication, some combination of factors? Again, we could lay the blame on the field of mental health as a whole; we still simply do not have the tools or the technology to help everyone. Elaine's suffering demonstrated that some people will make very little, if any, improvements in their lives. And for some of those who do, that change may be temporary. Until we develop new medications and therapeutic techniques, we have to shoulder the burden that there are people out there who will suffer for the duration of their lives. When you're a shrink, however, you can't ruminate on these shortcomings, because when a client/patient like Elaine walks out of the room, someone new walks in. You have to turn off your disappointment and snap into a new role—positive and confident— hoping to impact another life.

1 p.m.
Sex, Drugs, and Parents

Some clinicians estimate that there are well over 250 different approaches to therapy with children. Most of these have neither been formally researched nor officially validated as effective, yet they are practiced by mental health professionals all over the world. Why? While it is clear that the connection between a therapist and a child can in and of itself help promote psychological change, we don't really know what to *do* with kids. Furthermore, because children don't always know how to describe their distress levels and symptoms, accurate measurement of psychological improvement is difficult. To be blunt, many therapists working with children are simply winging it in the office and using very arbitrary measures of success.

Child therapy is somewhat of a misnomer because a parental figure or guardian is almost always involved in the treatment, at least for consultation and to facilitate follow-through of any therapeutic tasks outside of the office. *Parent/child therapy* is a more-accurate term for what goes on in a shrink's world. Sometimes, however, this is an arrangement that is met with at least some resistance, as parents very often see their child as "the problem." This viewpoint can often either directly or indirectly sabotage the work being done because there is a denial of responsibility on the parents' part. In fact, when I took an informal poll among mental health professionals, asking them what they considered the most difficult aspect of working with children, the answer was almost always the same: "The parents," they said. One colleague color-fully added, "The majority of kids I see would do so much better if their fucking parents would simply work with me and help out in the process instead of bitching about how 'gifted' their child is." In contrast, when asked about the most enjoyable aspect of child therapy, many replied simply, "The diversity." As one associate pointed out, "You're never just a 'therapist.' You have to talk to the parents and coach them, deal with the school system and make recommendations, give advice to the kids themselves, play games with them. It's so hard to get burned out because you're wearing so many hats." My own work with a very intriguing and quite unusual young man I'll call Jack highlights the many roles we play in child therapy.

Jack came to see me for several reasons. His father had made the initial call to my office for what he described as Jack's fear of school. Although Jack was extremely intelligent—his father reported that he had scored over 140 on a recent IQ test—he had very few friends and was often picked on by older adolescents. His parents were beginning the process of getting divorced, and Jack wanted nothing more than to remain at home studying computer software design, sculpting, opera, stock market trading, photography, and landscape architecture. He was rapidly approaching the literal title of Jack of all Trades.

When Jack entered my office suite for the first time he was dressed neatly in slacks and a sweater that suggested he was a private school student. His hair was perfectly combed and he had large, round spectacles that were likely endearing to adults but a dream weapon for bullies. As standard practice I address the child first, followed by the parent. This lets him know that he is the focus of my positive attention. "Hello, Jack. My name is Rob Dobrenski. And this, I assume, is your father?" *Role: child therapist.*

Jack, with a very small frame and even smaller hands, shook mine with a formality not usually seen in children. "Hello, Robert. How are you today?"

We know people ask that question all the time without even listening to the answer, but it crossed my mind that Jack wasn't making small talk. Maybe he really wanted to know how I was. Given that the six adult clients I had seen that day couldn't have cared less about how I was feeling, his query disarmed me.

"I'm . . . . good. Thank you for asking."

"That's nice," he said with a smile.

I explained to Jack's father, "Mr. Jack," that Jack and I would spend some time together talking, perhaps playing a game and getting to know each other a bit. Mr. Jack was a large, intimidating man dressed in an Armani suit with a massive gold watch on his right wrist. It was more like a small sundial than a standard timepiece.

"Fine, fine," he said, sounding somewhat dismissive and uninterested, and then sat down in one of the waiting room chairs and pulled out a copy of *The Economist* from his attaché case.

When Jack came into the office he looked around the room, slowly nodding his head and gently biting on his upper lip. "Yes, Robert," he said. "This is nice."

"I'm glad you like it. How about we have a seat on the floor and play a game, get to know each other." *Role: play date.*

"The floor?" Jack said suspiciously.

"Sure, why not? The carpet was recently shampooed."

Jack looked at the floor, then his slacks, then the floor again. "This is acceptable," he said, and sat down Indian-style.

I showed Jack the four or five games I had in the office and let him choose. "Connect Four," he said. "Strategy is an important skill to hone in one's youth."

When playing a game, I always let the child make the first move (although this is clearly disadvantageous if you hope to be triumphant at Connect Four). Ideally I let him win the first game or two to facilitate enjoyment of the experience so that he wishes to return. But I also like to win at least one game to gain insight as to how he handles disappointment. After I dropped the first six contests to Jack, I abandoned that goal.

"How much Hebrew do you know?" he asked as he tallied his eighth straight victory on a notepad he kept in his back pocket.

"Hebrew?"

"Yes, my mother said it would be nice if we spoke in Hebrew while we played."

The mom was definitely spot-on about the talking part. Play therapy ideally involves conversation about a child's difficulties while engaging in a playful activity. In fact, the game itself can serve as a medium for conversation. Some practitioners use board games such as the Talking, Feeling, and Doing Game (which basically involves sharing emotions while moving pieces around a board in a game format that doesn't allow anyone to win) to help a child express him- or herself in a nonthreatening environment.

In Jack's case, I was hoping to learn more about his fear of school (formally known as a specific phobia). Rather than sit him down on the couch and demand to know why he was afraid to go to school, we played and talked about his dominance at Connect Four while I periodically threw in questions and reassuring statements. "What are some of the things that kids your age hate about school?" and "I've helped other high school freshmen who have been nervous about school; maybe I could help you, too." This therapeutic style lets Jack know that sessions with me aren't all about him explaining or defending himself, and it tells him that he isn't the only person in the world with this sort of difficulty.

"I actually don't know any Hebrew," I confessed, wondering why the conversation wasn't about school but rather my language capabilities.

"You don't remember any from Hebrew school?"

"I never went to Hebrew school like you."

"But you're Jewish, right?"

"No, I'm not."

Jack recoiled in a combination of horror, confusion, and disgust, like I had just handed him a jar of urine. "Are you *Christian?*"

"No, I'm what they call 'agnostic.' Do you know what that means?"

"Everyone is either Jewish or Christian, unless you're a terrorist," he said with true fear in his voice.

"Actually, that's not true at all," I said, trying to be reassuring while attempting to resolve how someone so seemingly smart could have such a shortsighted view of religion. "There are lots of religions in the world."

"No, no, no! Terrorist!" Jack yelled as he got up and ran out of the office.

I pulled myself up from the floor and worked my way out to the waiting room, empty save for Jack cowering behind the large left leg of his very non-agnostic (and therefore non-terrorist) father.

"What the fuck is going on here?" said Mr. Jack.

"There was a misunderstanding with Jack. He thinks I'm a terrorist."

"Why would he think that? Are you from the Middle East?" he asked me, probably the whitest person in New York City.

"No, I'm agnostic."

"What the hell is agnostic?"

"It means that I'm not sure if there is a God or not. I think it's from the Greek word—"

"Jesus Christ, Dobrenski," said Mr. Jack, "this isn't religion class, it's counseling!"

"He asked me about my religion, and I don't lie to my clients. And I would appreciate it if you wouldn't use profanities or blaspheme in the waiting room."

"There's not even anyone here," said Mr. Jack.

"Robert's an anti-Semite!" said Jack.

"Jack, I am not an anti-Semite."

"Since when did you turn goyim, Dobrenski?" queried Mr. Jack.

"I didn't *turn* goyim, I've always been non-Jewish," I said, starting to feel defective for my non-chosen status.

"I guess it doesn't matter; just keep the whole anti-Messiah thing to a minimum in future sessions, okay?"

"I was just trying to do play therapy . . ."

By now Jack had heard enough and took off out of the office, into the elevator, and presumably onto Sixth Avenue.

"Wow, you really scared the shit out of him, huh?" said Mr. Jack with a combination of confusion and humor. "I'll talk to him and my bitch ex-wife, see if we can get him to come back again."

At that moment it occurred to me I could actually lose a client due to perceived potential for mass destruction.

Fortunately, Jack's mother called to tell me she explained to her son that I was not, in fact, a terrorist. I might even be a good person, she added. She went on to say that Jack had confirmed virtually everything she told him via Wikipedia and formal textbooks on religion and jihad and was, albeit with apprehension, willing to come in for a second appointment.

I explained to Mrs. Jack that it was imperative Jack return to school as quickly as possible. *Role: parent coach.* I was sure that his IQ would easily allow him to catch up on any missed schoolwork. She agreed, and said that she had already employed a reward system where Jack would receive extra time to plan his "upcoming spelunking trip" for each day he went to school. Apparently this was working extremely well, but with the divorce in the works she viewed it as important for Jack to continue to see me. She also said that Jack's father had begun to "write off" Jack, and that I shouldn't expect to see his father at future sessions.

In a strategic (or perhaps desperate) move to improve my therapeutic relationship with Jack, I chose to switch from Connect Four to UNO as the play-therapy game of choice. Mrs. Jack had told me that Jack was an avid UNO player. She also relayed that although he was only a freshman, he took many classes with seniors because of his advanced IQ, so I should be prepared to work with Jack's impressive verbal skills. It was then that I realized I should have spoken with Mrs. Jack prior to the first session.

A few minutes before Jack arrived for our second appointment, the guidance counselor from his school called. *Role: client liaison.* Having received permission from Jack's mother, he was reaching out to ensure that Jack would remain in treatment with me. Communicating with a child's school is common, especially when issues regarding grades, truancy, or specific behavior problems are involved.

"Does Jack really take senior-level classes?" I asked the counselor.

"Absolutely. He's such an amazing student and a really nice young man. He can certainly be naive at times, and has very few friends, but his heart is in a good place. God bless him."

When I hung up the phone I realized that I was running a few minutes late for session. I started to walk toward the waiting room. At the same time, I reached back for the UNO deck—and everything went white. A sharp pain shot up my lower back to my shoulders. I could feel my eyes glaze over with a white sheen. It was as if every nerve in my spine had caught on fire. This same injury had occurred years before, and I'd been diagnosed with "a bad spine, a chronic condition." Of course it had to reemerge right when I was about to meet with Jack.

I found myself on the floor flailing frantically in a pathetic attempt to massage my back muscles. Could any writer describe the enormity of this pain? Melville? Tolstoy? No one could come near it. Until you experience your flesh burning beneath your skin, you are living in ignorance. Sweet, beautiful ignorance.

When I was finally able to open my eyes I saw that I was a full ten minutes late. Jack had to have been wondering where I was. I needed to get to a standing position as soon as possible, but how? I reached up, grabbed the desk, and pushed down on it as hard as I could. Once I was on my feet the agony became bearable. I could feel the throbbing, but it wasn't making me cry, which is what I usually do when I'm in physical pain.

I made it out to the waiting room to find a somewhat confused and irritated patient. I apologized to Mrs. Jack, who stared at me, probably wondering why I was tilted slightly to the left.

"Come on in, buddy," I said to Jack. "Sorry to keep you waiting."

In the office I tried to explain the current situation. *Role: medical educator.* "Jack, I just hurt my back, and it's a little hard for me to sit on the floor and play cards. Do you mind if we use the table and I stand? Standing helps the pain. You'll have to shuffle, if that's okay?"

It's important to note that children do well with consistency and structure in therapy. Rules should be broken only when absolutely necessary.

"It can't be that bad, Robert," Jack said. "Can't you just tough it out the way my dad tells the football players on HDTV when they lie on the field, clutching their knees?"

Like his religious ignorance, I found it strange that Jack was taking AP Anatomy and Physiology and yet couldn't empathize with my physical issues.

"I'd really like to, but I can't. Let's just play the way I suggested and we'll talk about your mom and dad."

Jack let out an annoyed "Fine," and started to shuffle. Picking up the cards, I could feel the nerve endings in my back, screaming: *Surrender to us, Rob—relent. Nothing can stop us. You can't swallow enough Vicodin to calm this pain.*

Within reason, children do better in therapy if they see you as mentally strong and in control. Thus, I didn't ask Jack to pick up the cards for me even though I knew I wouldn't be able to bend over too many times.

"Tell me about your time with Dad this weekend."

"Fine."

Open-ended questions are the interrogative method of choice, and therapists shouldn't be afraid to push the envelope a bit.

"That's great, but tell me about it."

"Well, we went to dinner at Olive Garden with Dad's new girlfriend. Then we played Halo."

"You and Dad?"

"No, me and Angie."

"That's Dad's new girlfriend?"

"Yeah, she's awesome. She bought me candy and got me a bunch of flash drives from the audiovisual department at school."

"Oh, so she works at a school?"

"No, we go to the same school. Angie graduates in a few months. It just sucks because we have a few classes together, so next year she won't be there."

Right then, as I reached for my third "Draw Four" in a row, trying to process the fact that Jack's dad was actually *dating* one of his son's classmates, the pain shot up and then down my back, and I couldn't hold back an unusually girlish and shrill scream.

"What's wrong? You don't approve of Angie?"

"No, no, it's not that. It's my back."

"Liar! You hate Angie! *Mommmm!*"

In what was starting to become a standard ritual for ending our sessions, Jack ran out of the office. I slowly and gingerly followed him into the waiting room, mentally preparing for another lecture from a distressed parent.

"Jack ran into the bathroom. He told you about Angie?" says Mrs. Jack.

"Yes, it was just a case of bad timing. I hurt my back, and I just winced at the moment he revealed that she was, um, younger than what one would traditionally expect."

"That's fine, Doctor. Are you okay?"

"I've been better," I confessed. "Are you okay with your son spending time with Angie?"

It is important to always find out parental reactions to new and important people in a child's life. *Role: parent therapist.*

"If you want the truth, she's an eighteen-year-old hussy. But she adores Jack and can't spend enough of Mr. Jack's money. So that makes me happy."

"I don't want to imply that there's anything wrong with it, but I'd like to spend some time with Jack discussing nontraditional relationships and how it impacts him, if that's all right with you."

"That would be great. I don't think you want to start that right now, though. He's very protective of Angie, and I'm guessing you really upset him."

"I know," I said sadly. "I've been doing that quite a bit lately."

"Next week, then?" asked Mrs. Jack.

"Absolutely," I said with a forced and pained smile.

Closing the door behind her, I heard Jack come out of the bathroom. "He hates Angie!" he yelled. "I'm not going back, ever! No. More. Robert! No. More. Robert!" Jack chanted over and over as his voice and footsteps slowly dissipated.

After our misunderstanding regarding his classmate and potential stepmother, Angie, our relationship had suffered a rift. Therefore, the goal of the next session, despite the agony, was to reestablish the therapeutic alliance. In other words, I had to get the extremely bright and interpersonally sensitive Jack to like me again—assuming he had liked me to begin with—and to have confidence that I could help him. Research suggests that a strong therapeutic connection is perhaps the best predictor of a positive outcome in treatment.

"Jack, let's talk about what happened last time."

"I'd like that very much. But we should converse as adults," Jack said as he sat with perfect posture on the therapy couch, dressed in Perry Ellis.

"That would be . . . lovely," I said, realizing that if I'd had Jack's posture as a teenager, I probably wouldn't have my current back problems. "Shall I speak first?"

"Actually," Jack said, "Mom explained your malady to me, and I looked it up on WebMD. How do you intend to mitigate your ailment?"

"Mitigate?"

"Yes," Jack said. "The SATs are coming up in three years, and there are some fascinating words related to back injuries. Your pain is my gain."

"Well, good. Let's not worry about my back; let's talk about you and me. Do you understand now that I don't dislike Angie?"

"Yes, I am able to descry that."

Could Jack be the spawn of Merriam and/or Webster?

"Mom told me that you really like Angie," I said.

"She's great. I know it's a little different, or at least that's what my classmates tell me. But when she's around I get to see my dad. I have to take what I can get."

Given that his dad was probably spending most of his time engrossed in his new love interest, I was very impressed with Jack's perspective.

"Robert," Jack said, a bit anxiously, "there's something that my mom told me to speak to you about."

"Great. Do you want to play some UNO while we talk?"

"No, please. Adult dialogue today."

"All right, then," I said, somewhat relieved that I didn't have to get down on the floor again. "Go ahead."

"Well, my non-Dungeons and Dragons colleagues are really interested in girls and sex. I think I like girls, but I might like guys too. I find both sexes somewhat sexually appealing."

Afraid to move a muscle lest I let out another scream of back pain, I spoke. "So you're not quite sure of your sexuality yet? Am I getting that right?"

"Yes," he said, staring at the floor, seemingly guilt-ridden.

"You know, Jack, I don't think that's anything to be ashamed of, but it looks as though that's the way you feel."

"Normally I wouldn't care; it's just that everyone else seems so sure about their sexuality."

"Do you get a lot of peer pressure to like girls, Jack?"

"I wouldn't say a lot; more like a modicum."

"Okay, a 'modicum' of peer pressure, then."

"Shouldn't I just know what I am?"

"Actually, I don't think you should have to know for sure, Jack. It's okay to be curious. Maybe if we talked about it during our sessions, you might develop a sense of your sexual preference, but I don't think you should pressure yourself to know right at this moment. And whatever you do decide about your sexual preference is okay. You need to know that." *Role: sex educator.*

"Some of my friends aren't virgins and they want me to have sexual relations as well."

"Are you considering becoming sexually active?" Because there is no magical age when a person should start having sex, it is important to convey a calm tone of acceptance, indicating that whatever the answer is, the client will not be judged.

"No, I'm not really considering it. Should I be?"

"Do you think you're ready for that?" Although I had an opinion, I find it is generally a good idea to let the client think things through and process his own opinion before hearing mine.

"Um, not really. I don't know much about sex, actually, other than seeing *Knocked Up* four times and looking at a few dirty magazines that my friend has."

"I think you answered your own question, then. I know some people your age are sexually active, but that doesn't mean that you should be if you don't feel ready. Personally, I think your age group is a little young for sex, but that's not for me to decide. Only you can know when the time is right. I can help you figure it out, but you'll ultimately make that decision for yourself."

"So, instead of playing UNO, are you saying we can talk about sex?"

"If that's what is on your mind, I don't see why not."

"Great! Mom will be so happy. Ever since she and Dad broke up, she's been afraid that she's going to have to be the one to teach me everything. Now you can do it for her. Robert, you are truly a sagacious man."

As he stepped out of the office that day, I realized I would probably never hear those words again.

Prior to the next session with my Sex Machine in Training, Mrs. Jack faxed me a note, apparently in an effort to help me prepare my lesson plans:

Dear Dr. Dobrenski,

Please know how happy I am that you will assist Jack in learning about "the birds and the bees." I never did find out which I am, a bird or a bee! ☺ Since his father and I divorced, I believe that Jack is lacking a strong male role model, and his questions regarding sex are numerous. Please be sure to cover the following topics in your upcoming session:

Heterosexual intercourse
Homosexual intercourse
Light and heavy petting
Mainstream sexual positions
Orgasms (singular, multiple, and faked)
Condoms and other forms of contraception
Sex toys
Hard swaps and soft swaps

Common terms Jack might find on UrbanDictionary.com (e.g.,
Dirty Sanchez)
The purpose of AdultFriendFinder.com

Have a great day!
Mrs. Jack

With this new information, I could only assume that Mrs. Jack wanted her son to not only be knowledgeable about sex, but highly skilled at it as well.

What made my task even easier was Jack's copy of the *Kama Sutra*, which he had tucked under his arm as he sat ever-so-properly on the therapy couch. "Mom got it from Amazon with free shipping!"

This entire scenario created a moral dilemma, one which many therapists experience daily. We know that there are children even younger than Jack who are having sex, many of them unsafely and without any real education on the matter. If Jack didn't learn about sex and its ramifications from me, where would he learn it? Not from his father. In science class from some giant poster depicting a fallopian tube? On the street? By trial and error? Mrs. Jack knew the score as well, and because I had a good, albeit sometimes tenuous, working relationship with him, she asked me to give him correct information so that he was not left to his own devices. In many ways this made her a great parent who clearly didn't have her head in the sand regarding how the world worked. And yet did I really want to promote, either directly or inadvertently, sexuality to someone who was not psychologically developed enough to fully understand all of its nuances?

Clinical wisdom suggests that when unsure how to proceed with social concerns such as sex, drugs, or alcohol, a mental health professional should present the facts truthfully, while maintaining appropriate involvement with parental figures. This helps to prevent delivering your own specific agenda and allows the parents to weigh in with their belief systems.

"Jack, I know your mom bought that book for you, but I'd like to talk about it with her before you and I take a look at it."

"Why is that, Robert?"

"Well, many people think that book is for adults only, and I'd like us to talk about the basics of human sexuality before discussing . . . more advanced matters."

"Hmmm," Jack said contemplatively.

"Let's talk about sexuality for a little while and then I'd like to sit down with your mom and tell her about our discussion, if that's all right with you."

"That is acceptable," says Jack.

"Right. Good. Now, do you know what sex is for?"

"To perpetuate the species," he responded confidently, as if he had just read a biology textbook. "And I'm told it's fun. Is it fun?" he asked.

When therapists don't want to answer a question, they should feel free to say so. But a good rule of thumb is not to lie. While children do not necessarily benefit from hearing every single detail of life, baldly false statements destroy a relationship that is ideally built on trust and will ultimately undermine the therapist's credibility.

"That's right, it is to procreate. And yes, most people find sex to be fun."

"Most people? Not everyone?"

"Well, it is very important that sex occur between people who actually want to have sex with each other. Consensual. People are sometimes forced to have sex, which is not only not fun, but hurts them, both physically and psychologically. Does that make sense?"

Explaining sex to a teenager whose vocabulary is at the master's degree level proved to be daunting.

"Like the whole 'you can't touch me there' thing?"

"Exactly."

"But it can be fun, and that's why people are always doing it?" he asked.

"For many people, that is why they do it, yes."

"I see," he said, satisfied with my answers. "Now, moving on. I have read that this can be done orally, vaginally, and anally. Is that correct, Robert?"

I have worked with sexual abuse victims, sexual offenders, sexual offenders' spouses, and countless people on sexual idiosyncrasies without batting an eyelash, but seeing a fourteen-year-old in a blue blazer with a crest on it, speaking like Dr. Ruth, made me feel beads of perspiration form on my forehead.

"Right," I stammered slightly. "That is correct."

"Why are some people gay and some straight?"

I sensed that Jack's questions might be getting progressively more difficult.

"That's actually a question that no one truly knows the answer to. Some people think that people are born homosexual or heterosexual, and some people think it's a choice that people make."

"And you, Robert? What do you think?"

Did I murder someone? Am I on trial here? Again, the rule: Do. Not. Lie.

"Let me put it to you this way: The majority of the people I help and the people I know in my life consider themselves straight. But I also know people who are gay, and most of them have told me that they always knew they were gay, that they felt it from a young age."

"Does that make me a freak because I don't know?"

"Absolutely not," I said, going into reassurance mode. "Like we discussed, it's not required that you know anything right now."

"Maybe I'm bisexual."

"Maybe you are. Would you be okay with that?"

"My gay friend said that I have to make a choice. He said it's like having a mullet: either let it grow out or cut it. I don't even understand what that means."

"Some people feel very strongly that everyone should have a specific sexual preference, whether it's for a male or a female partner. But that doesn't make it a fact. It might be hard to understand this now, but sex is a very subjective concept, and there aren't any definitive answers. You will decide what is best for you."

"Thank you, Robert. But if I'm going to make the choice myself, why is my mother paying you?"

He might as well have added the word *Checkmate!* to the end of that query.

"Because she and I think that I might be able to help guide you along as you make decisions about sex. Do you agree?"

"I do, but I'm using 'concur' now. That's my word of the week."

"Well I'm glad you concur."

Jack took out a sheet of paper, which turned out to be the original missive that Mrs. Jack had faxed over. "Oh, Robert!" he said, frustrated. "We've hardly covered any of these topics, you still need to meet with Mom, and we're running out of time!"

"All in good time, buddy. We'll get to it all soon enough. Be patient and it will all work out fine."

"Okay," he said with a small smile, which helped me to feel more at ease and, ever so briefly, like a competent therapist. "I'm going to let you and Mom have some adult time. You two have a nice chat. Next week we'll talk about masturbation—can we agree to that?"

"Um, sure, absolutely."

"Good, because I need to become more of an expert at it. That would be fantastic!"

The brief feeling of confidence suddenly flew out the window.

After many months of working with Jack, I was able to draw a number of definitive conclusions:

- Jack is an unusual young man.
- His IQ is significantly higher than mine.
- His intellectual understanding of sexuality without any life experience can alienate him from other adolescents.
- He is made fun of for having a stepmother figure who attends the same school.
- His father is mostly absent from his life, but his mother, while a bit unorthodox, is actively involved.
- His use of words like *vicissitudes* and *sequacious* as opposed to words like *yo, dude,* and *fo' shizzle* make him appear awkward in the eyes of his peers.

Many of these issues brought his mood down. But his intelligence and instincts told him that he was a good person who cared about others, and this ultimately seemed to help carry him through days when he was feeling blue. When he needed an additional boost, I came into play, basically pulling answers out of the air for his plethora of questions, as many child therapists do.

"Robert, I feel a bit torpid today, and I'm not quite sure what to do about it. May I enlist your help?"

"Of course, Jack. I'll do my best. Tell me about what you're experiencing and let's see what we can do."

When working with children and adolescents, it is important to convey a confidence that, regardless of the problem, you can be of help. *Whatever is going on, we can handle it* is the message.

"I know I'm not depressed, just somewhat down. Dysthymic, perhaps? Is that the proper term?"

Unsurprisingly that was the *exact* term.

"I see. A case of the blahs?" Why Jack sounded like the DSM-IV and I was using words that sounded like baby talk shouldn't have surprised me after so many months together. But it did.

"Exactly. Do you have any specific coping strategies that you can pass along?"

"Well let me ask you a question first. When you feel dysthymic, do you tend to be . . . sedentary?"

"Oh, yes."

"Okay, this is very common. You need to know that a case of the blues and inactivity often go hand in hand. They can be the best of friends." Like an idiot I crossed two fingers to show how connected depression and inactivity can be, just in case the boy genius in front of me didn't understand this basic premise.

"So you are saying that I should become more active to help my mood, Robert?"

"Yes, that is exactly right. Additionally, research has shown that people tend to do best when they engage in activities that are not only pleasurable, but also have a high degree of mastery. You know, things you're good at." Meanwhile I'm thinking *Please don't ask about masturbation again.*

"Yes, I am familiar with the term 'mastery.' "

"Yes. Yes, of course you are. You can remember the key terms of 'mastery,' 'activity,' and 'pleasure' with the simple acronym MAP."

"Indeed," Jack said. "I think I prefer PAM, however. That's my aunt's name."

"Okay, that sounds good to me."

"Or how about AMP, as in 'I'm amped to beat this dysthymic mood.' "

"Any of those are good." *Does his brain ever stop working?*

"Or even PMA, for 'Plan Many Activities.' Yes, that one is good too! Do you want to write all of these down for your other clients?"

"I'm hoping I can remember those," I said, knowing full well that I would frantically scratch out all of those mnemonics the moment Jack left the session.

"Good. I'm glad to hear you haven't lost your memory yet."

"Why would I lose my memory?"

"Dementia of the Alzheimer's type probably isn't far off, you know."

So in addition to reading the dictionary, he had studied psychiatry terminology as well as learning about the onset and perhaps even the progression of brain disease.

"I'm glad to hear that you are concerned about my memory, but Alzheimer's is extremely rare before the age of fifty, and isn't usually a concern before the age of sixty-five."

"Robert, one day you'll realize that thirty years to get to sixty-five is such a short time, given the grand scheme of our universe. I will see you next week." He might as well have showered me with rose petals or touched my head in a form of religious blessing.

As he exited I realized how exhausting he could be at times. And depressing. That night I craved a few Massive Pints of Ale to help with my own dysthymia.

As the years went on and Jack got older, approaching seventeen, he improved. He used MAP or PAM or AMP or whatever it was that he ultimately decided upon. He used his sex knowledge to impress girls and develop a few friendships, although he still wasn't sure if it was boys he wished to impress instead. And he continued to accept the fact that his father was going to have an unorthodox romantic relationship and that he and Jack would probably never be very close. These improvements were all things that pleased both him and his mother.

It was about this time that I broached the concept of ending therapy. Mrs. Jack had an immediate question. "In many ways you're a father to him. Can he handle not seeing you anymore?" *Role: father figure.*

"Yes, I believe he can. We'll taper off slowly, and he will know that the door will always be open for him."

She paused for a few moments, her eyes looking slightly to the right. "All right," she finally said. "It's just that Jack still has so many questions to ask you."

"I understand. But what's important here is that Jack will *always* have lots of questions. That's part of his hard-wiring and it won't ever change. It's not a bad thing. He is keenly aware that I'm not an authority on so many things. He also knows to talk to you, use the library, go online, and speak with his new friends. He will constantly have a thirst for knowledge but will develop more and more ways to have his questions answered."

"Do you think he's . . . gay?" she whispered, despite the fact that the office waiting area was empty.

"I'm not sure. To be honest I don't think he needs to know that right now, and I think he should take his time figuring that out. I will always be willing to talk to him about what it all means, but there's no point in slapping a label on him just for the sake of identity. If it takes years for him to be sure, so be it."

Mrs. Jack was very satisfied with that answer. "Can he at least ask you a bunch of things in your final sessions with him?"

"Of course he can," I said.

I planned our last few meetings as a general discussion about how to make a greater-than-academic sense of the world. Jack instead used our last few hours together running through a series of rapid-fire questions:

Robert, what's it like to kiss a girl?

Robert, would you kiss a boy if he asked you really, really nicely?

Robert, if I were pro-choice, would that isolate me from my Republican identity?

Robert, could you please resolve the nature/nurture debate for me?

Robert, my dentist died of autoerotic asphyxiation. What does that mean?

Robert, why are you named Robert?

Robert Robert Robert Robert . . .

To this day I still wake up some nights hearing my name repeated over and over in his voice.

I was always honest with Jack, even when I refused to answer a question. *No, Jack, I will not elaborate on my sexual fantasies . . . Yes, I know we agreed that everyone has them, but that doesn't change the fact that I would prefer not to share them with you.*

We then agreed to taper down our sessions to once every three weeks, rather than simply halt the therapeutic process altogether. This is a common practice and helps clients, especially young ones, become acclimated to a new routine. During times that had normally been reserved for appointments with me, Jack would engage in mostly academic pursuits (e.g., attend a conference on nuclear fission or win a calculus competition against college-aged mathematics majors). And during those times, I actually missed him. As frustrating as Jack could be, I truly enjoyed trying to pass along the knowledge I had gained over the years. I was relishing the fatherly role.

There is potential danger when a therapist has some of his personal needs satisfied through work. While there is nothing wrong with enjoying the job, the contentment should come from the client's improved quality of life. In graduate school, professors warned us to keep tabs on our behavior with each client so we didn't ever cross boundaries. For example, therapists who more carefully choose their clothing on days they see a certain client are at risk for putting that person's treatment in jeopardy. They are starting to cross a line toward favoritism, sexual attraction, or a desire to be liked by the client, however subtle it may seem. This can lead therapists to move the work in directions that aren't always in the client's best interests and thus needs to be avoided.

That being said, therapy doesn't exist in a vacuum. Therapists have reactions, thoughts, and feelings about their clients. In and of themselves they are not a problem; it's what we do with them that matters.

The best way to prevent the problem of having personal needs met through the clients is by paying close attention to both your own behavior and the therapeutic process. This helps to ensure that the needs of the patient are being met. If it's true that everyone has a need to be a parent, then I'm likely to meet that need through my work, especially since I don't have my own children. So I needed to strongly monitor myself and my emotions, and talk to Jack's mother and possibly future stepmother about what occurred in session. I would also occasionally discuss the issues with Dr. Pete (behind closed doors, of course, so Pete's Xanax use could be kept to a minimum). This helped to ensure that I didn't give Jack preferential treatment or guide the therapy in a direction that helped me to feel "fatherly" for my own sake.

Pete is particularly good at noticing therapists' personal motivations in their work, so I wanted to discuss the imminent completion of Jack's treatment.

"So, Jack was reporting anxiety because he feels distant from his father. How did you feel when he said that?" Pete asked.

"I felt bad for him. I wanted to help him on that."

"That's it? You felt bad for him? What else?"

"Like what?"

"You didn't feel any sense of competition with his father? It didn't occur to you that maybe you could get him to like you more than his father by doing a particularly good job that session?"

"It's pretty easy to be liked more than his father."

"Come on, you know the kid wants a relationship with him."

"True. Of course it occurred to me, but that's not where my thoughts predominantly were. I was disappointed."

"How so?" Pete asked.

"Well, he told me at the end of the last session that he got a 99 percent on his biochemical engineering test, and he usually gets 100 percent. I was hoping to impart some sagacious, fatherly wisdom about how no one is perfect, and that he can still be a huge success."

"Okay, so your needs and his didn't match up."

"Not initially, no."

"Were you able to put your own shit aside?"

"Yes, absolutely," I said.

"How?"

"I'm not sure; I guess just through recognizing it. I knew I could have strong-armed him into talking about the test, but that would have been more for me than him."

"Pretty simple, no?" Pete asked.

He was right. And sober. Similar to my discussions with Dr. Charles, positive results don't always take place through trenchant insights on the part of the therapist. It's often simply a matter of asking a few questions and adding some observations.

Almost three years after I had met Jack, it was finally time to say good-bye. Of course, Jack couldn't allow it to be as simple as that, however.

"Robert, it was very kind of you to take the time out of your schedule to work with me on my psychological distress. You helped me to get back to school, feel more comfortable with sex, and accept my parents' divorce. I have a few more friends now and you are responsible for that. You are a good man and deserve success in this life. As an agnostic, you may or may not believe in future lives. If they exist, then I hope you find happiness there as well."

With that and a firm, confident handshake, he left the office without looking back.

It's very often difficult to quantify what a therapist does, especially when working with children. At that moment, though, I remembered something a professor told me about child therapy outcome: "There are hundreds of ways to do child therapy, but the good ones all have two ingredients in common: talk, and a safe therapeutic relationship. If you can provide both of those things, there is so much you can do for a child."

It all clicked right then and there. Despite my innumerable issues and neuroses and problems in the office with Jack, and although I sometimes drove him to the point of never wanting to see me again, I was a stable force in his life. He needed me when his parents were splitting up, when his dad took on a new girlfriend, when he couldn't ask anyone about his sexual orientation. Even though I got in my own way more often than not, I still managed to be there, working with him through the awkward phase of developing from a child to a young man, and that's why our work together accomplished a great deal. Fortunately, Jack is now a happier person because of it.

2 p.m.

The Pain We Believe Will Never Cease

Because our brains are designed to try to make sense of everything that happens, to create meaning, to put things into a context, grief work is all about processing. It's taking every thought and feeling you have about your loss and articulating it, acknowledging it, letting it sit with you. I explain to clients that while it may initially appear desirable to try to "forget and move on" as quickly as possible, this is not the way the brain is constructed. I sometimes use an analogy involving a simple, old-fashioned toy to help drive this point home:

> Pretend that you're the paddle and the rubber ball is your feelings. When something bad happens to us, our natural instinct is to try to push the bad feelings away. It's like we hit the rubber ball as hard as possible to make it vanish, but the harder we hit it, the stronger and faster the ball bounces back. It's like the ball doesn't want to leave us. Grief feelings are like that. They need to sit still and be understood. The good news is that if we talk about your feelings, we can make many negative aspects of the ball disappear.

No one can definitively articulate how this process works—at least, not yet. But the articulation and processing changes the pain. It reshapes it, makes it more manageable.

Grief is somewhat of a catchall term used to describe any sort of loss. Traditionally people think that one grieves when he loses a family member or close relationship due to death (and with 56 million deaths per year, this is a common phenomenon). However, our minds are capable of forming attachments to many things because they are part of our identity. People grieve when a relationship ends, as I did with Janet, or when a job is terminated. We grieve that loss because part of who we are has been taken away.

Even positive events can provoke a grief response: Graduating from high school is an achievement and stepping-stone to other things, but those who have finished their education sometimes report feelings of grief as they leave an important time in their development. Even formerly obese people who have changed their lifestyle in order to lose weight will sometimes say: "I feel like I've lost a friend. Food was what I turned to when life was hard. I have other things to do that for me now, but there are many times when I find myself grieving the loss of my relationship with food."

Because grief is a mostly universal experience, an occupational hazard of being a therapist is to assume that you can simply use your own history to understand the feelings of another. While using personal experience can be a barometer to approximate what a client might be experiencing, grief reactions are so complex and multifaceted that no one can truly say "I know how you feel," even if such a response comes from a place of sympathy.

My first experience directly working with grief came early on in my private practice. The client, a fifty-nine-year-old woman whom I'll call Sara, made an appointment with me at the suggestion of her physician. Her husband, whom I'll call Mike, had died of cancer just two months prior. The cancer had moved rapidly and he had succumbed to it within a few months. Since his death, Sara had been unable to concentrate on her work, which led to poor reviews from her employers. She had lost twenty pounds due to not eating, and her sleep, when it came, was fitful. She didn't see her friends and was having crying spells throughout the day. She had been married for almost forty years to Mike. That happened to be nine years longer than I had been alive, and yet it was my job to provide her with the wisdom and insights to piece her life back together.

Sara's difficulties highlight an important point around grief: It's not very common for people to seek therapy for the death of a spouse. Because sadness is considered a "normal" response to a loss, many do not seek professional help for it. When clients do come in, it is often because some aspect of their functioning is being compromised. For many the feelings themselves might not drive them to seek help, but if their job is suffering or their relationships are being damaged, this might push them to see a professional.

Sara grew up in a Southern, African-American home where emphasis was placed on keeping your feelings in. Talking about emotional pain was considered a sign of weakness. "Pull yourself up by your bootstraps" was the mantra in her family's culture. In fact, Sara wouldn't have even considered seeing a therapist had she not been having trouble at work. And while her doctor was willing to prescribe an antidepressant if she didn't improve over time, he insisted that she try therapy first.

Sara was a very religious woman. A strong Christian background had led to her firm relationship with God. She presented herself at her first session very formally in a proud business suit; clearly, dignity was at the top of her priority list.

Unless you share personal information with clients, they are forced to make assumptions about you. Whether Sara was particularly shrewd or simply lucky, she deduced facts about me. My New Jersey accent, my semi-casual attire of khakis and a button-down shirt, with the sleeves slightly rolled, my relative youth and inexperience. She used these markers to make decisions. "I suspect you are not a man of God."

Is she attempting to assess if I could be of use to her? Is it a way to simply avoid talking about the real issue: her? It was perhaps both.

"What makes you say that?" I asked.

"Modern-day Northerners don't have that deep connection with the Lord—at least not in my experience. Especially younger people."

I told her that while I didn't believe that was entirely true, she was correct about me. However, being an agnostic, I explained, didn't mean I was godless. "Do you think that might cause a problem in our work together?" I asked.

"I don't really know what to think anymore, Doctor. Your husband is one day healthy, one day sick, one day dead. Everything changes in heartbeats. But I can't lose my job, and my friends tell me that I need to 'get better,' whatever that means. So I'd like to hear how you might be able to help me."

I explained to her my take on bereavement work: "This might sound like a foreign idea, but the more you can share your feelings about what has happened to you, the more confident I am that you can feel better. Our minds are equipped with what I like to think of as filing cabinets for our emotions. When we've experienced a loss, we lose control of the cabinet, and all of the feelings are exposed. That's why people who are grieving have nightmares and can't concentrate. The feelings become intrusive; you can't open and close the drawers at your choosing. Therapy helps people get that control back. The goal of treatment isn't to forget; far from it. It's to have a greater say in *when* you think about your loss, and for *how long*. You'll always come back to those feelings, but they won't control you as they do now. You'll decide when the filing cabinet opens and closes."

Sara looked at me suspiciously. "I can't ever see that happening."

"I think I understand," I said. "And many people say that. They can't even imagine feeling anything that is different from right now. But if you work very hard I strongly believe that things will change."

She knew that her current attempts to feel better weren't helping. "I will try," she said.

"That's all I ask."

Our initial sessions were clunky. Given her background, Sara didn't open up freely. She was a very private, formal person. When I asked her direct questions she would provide short answers. "How did you feel yesterday?" "Okay." When I asked her to expand on her feelings, she often replied that she didn't know how. If you're a social, outgoing, or type A personality, this can be frustrating. But if you remember that the client is battling not only intense psychological pain but also working against the very grain of their psyche, it's easier to be patient.

When clients are not processing their emotions through traditional dialogue, I sometimes ask them to tell me a story.

"Tell me about your first date with Mike."

"We went out to dinner and to the movies."

"No, I mean *tell* me about it."

"What do you mean?"

"Pretend you're a teenager and you're writing about the date in your diary. Say what you would write."

"I can't."

"Sara, please try. It's very important."

She sighed and looked down at her fingers, which looked sinewy and older than they needed to be. There was a silver, antique wedding band on her finger that she twirled around. She smiled, and let out a small, embarrassed laugh. "Dr. Dobrenski, the truth is that we didn't get along all that well on our first date. He was late, a major no-no for me and my family, and he didn't apologize right away. I only decided to continue with the evening because he practically begged me to go to dinner at some fancy restaurant with him, for which he had reservations. He wasn't a great conversationalist, either; he talked mostly about himself."

"Was he very self-absorbed?" I asked.

She paused. "No, I don't think it was that. I think he was nervous. We were set up by a mutual friend, and I think he didn't want me to say negative things about him to her. But I wasn't impressed."

"What made you decide to go out with him again?"

Another small smile crossed her face. "Oh, he was relentless, although to this day I have no idea why. For whatever reason he was smitten, and he sent me flowers for four straight days. Roses, big red roses. It seemed like the buds got bigger and the stems got longer each time. How a nineteen-year-old college kid afforded that was beyond me."

"So he broke your spirit with roses," I said, rubbing my chin in a faux-serious way. And her smile grew. *Why couldn't I have won over Janet in the same way?* I actually envied Mike at that moment, having a woman feel so strongly for him.

"Yes you could say that. On the next date he was on time, much more attentive, and a total gentleman. He told me that I looked beautiful, and that people only deserve one more chance. He promised that he wouldn't ever be late again. And he wasn't." Sara looked down at her fingers again, twirled the band that hadn't left her finger in over forty years, and sniffled.

"What does it feel like to tell me that story?" I asked.

"I miss him. So, so much. It's like I'm dead too." She looked up toward the ceiling. "Why did you leave?"

As our sessions continued Sara continued to lay out her feelings. I always encouraged her to say more, to process her life with Mike, to get the filing cabinet in order. "What was that like? Tell me about that. What do you feel as you describe it to me?"

Sara would sometimes ask questions of me. "Why do we grieve? What's its purpose?" This is a common query from those who are grappling with loss.

"I see it as a very natural, very painful state that is part of our evolution. I think it's our way of knowing what's truly important to us, so that people come together and form communities. It's our signal that we cared about something very deeply. If you didn't feel pain when Mike died, what would that suggest?"

"That I didn't love him, I suppose."

"Right. Now some people don't grieve in the pure sense, especially if the relationship with the person who died was complicated or conflicted. They may not be sure how to feel. Some people feel guilt, others anger, and some people feel relieved."

"I wish I could feel some relief," she said.

"Do these sessions help at all?"

"Sometimes I wonder, but usually I think they do. I'm not sure why."

"You're processing," I said. "Your mind is putting all of these events into a context that makes sense. If you keep going with this, I'm confident we'll continue to see gains." This is not something I would have said to David, the man who suffered from severe OCD, but it came easily when speaking with Sara. She was on track for success.

Progress in therapy isn't linear, however, and Sara would have weeks where she felt worse. Sometimes she would shut down and be unwilling or unable to add much to the work. I could sometimes see the frustration in her silence, her face twisted as the thoughts and emotions roiled around inside her.

Once a therapeutic relationship has been firmly established, it is important for a therapist to be gentle as he continues to elicit emotions. Some practitioners will choose to let a client remain silent, allowing her to speak when she is ready. After a few months I concluded that Sara's connection to me and the treatment was strong enough that she could be pushed—that silences could be challenged.

"Sara, what's going through your mind right now?"

"Nothing."

"Come on, talk to me. Say what's going through your mind."

"It's . . . hard."

"I know," I said.

This is a critical error made by some mental health professionals. As Dr. Charles had taught me, one of the goals for therapists is to "walk in the client's shoes" as closely as possible. Approaching this ideal helps the client to feel understood—that at some level, the therapist "gets it." But because one can never truly understand another person's emotional state, even if a similar emotional state has been shared, saying "I know" or perhaps even worse, "I know how you feel," is inherently invalidating. It implies that the individual's experience is no longer unique.

"How do you know?" Sara asked.

"I don't," I said. "I'm sorry for saying that."

"Have you lost a spouse?" Sara asked, a hint of anger coming into her voice.

"No, I've never been married."

"Right, you told me that. So you can't *know*, can you?"

"Again, I apologize. And the reality is that even if I had lost a spouse, that wouldn't mean I know every feeling you have. Your experience is your own."

"That's right, it's my own!" she said. "I'll bet you've never lost anyone in your life."

"That's not fair," I said.

"Then tell me. Who? Who died?"

There are countless articles, book chapters, and lecture series on the topic of therapist self-disclosure. Theories range from complete silence to sharing many aspects of the self. There is no consensus within the field, no clear-cut way of measuring if and when it is appropriate to talk about oneself. One professor, however, summed up self-disclosure for me concisely: *If you think telling the client something about yourself will help him/her, if it's not about some cathartic moment for you or a way to get your own therapy on your client's time and dime, then do so.*

"Who?!" she repeated.

"My sister. My sister died."

Sara leaned back into the couch, studying me, wondering perhaps if I was lying to her. "When?"

"A long time ago. Twelve years."

"I'm sorry," Sara said.

"Thank you."

"No, I mean I'm sorry for raising my voice, for making assumptions. All of my friends, all of whom are still married, keeping telling me to be strong, that they know what I'm going through. They don't know anything about my pain."

"You're right, they don't. Is that what this was about? Another person telling you he knows what you're feeling?"

"I think so. Can I ask how your sister died?"

"Before I answer, do you mind telling me why you'd like to know that?"

"My husband was a young man. He shouldn't have left. It's not like losing a parent to old age. This feels . . . unnatural. Losing a sibling seems similar in some ways."

One of the benefits of group therapy is the concept of universality. Through being with other people, clients can come to understand that they are not alone. *Other people have had similar experiences, and, while not identical to mine, these experiences help me to feel less alone with this.*

Sara needed me to give her some universality.

"She died of a drug overdose," I said. "She was an addict."

Sara looked away from me. She held a moment or two of what seemed to be deep thought. "How did you get through that?"

"By doing exactly what I'm asking of you," I said. "I talked about every feeling and thought I had about her. I even wrote her a letter."

"And what about your parents?"

"They . . . I don't think they've ever really recovered."

"I hear that losing a child is a pain that can't ever be eased," Sara said.

"I wonder about that as well. I think they each made the mistake I've pushed you not to do: trying to block it out, to not think about it, to suppress it. The pain was too much for them to process."

"Are you angry with her? Your sister?"

"I was at the time. I was angry that she did that to me, and to her son, and to our parents."

"I'm angry at Mike for leaving me," Sara said. "He took great care of himself and I know, intellectually, that it's not his fault. But I'm still angry."

"Tell me more. Say more about being angry." But at that moment it was very difficult to concentrate on what Sara was going to say next. I was now mentally caught up in my own life: the call to my college apartment from my stepfather to tell me my sister had died; my roommate wrapping his arms around me in a bear hug when I told him what had happened; the days and then weeks and then months and then years of seeing my mother cry and listening to my dad change the subject when the word "Laura" came up. Within seconds I was starting to relive moments of me screaming at a girlfriend for smoking pot, or my mother walking around the house like a robot, putting a hammer in the refrigerator and a bottle of ketchup in the garage, her mind not one with her surroundings. My filing cabinet had flown open and I quickly needed to close the drawers for Sara's sake. This was her time, not mine.

I told myself that later that night I would go home and open up my mental cabinet; I'd allow the rubber ball to sit against the paddle. I'd think about my sister's death, cry for a bit, call my mom and let her know if I had helped anyone that day, and then I'd shut it down. Like I had told Sara, you never forget; you just gain more control over the memories.

It was as if Sara could see the wheels spinning in my head. "You went back to a dark time, didn't you?"

"Yes. I'm sorry. That's not your concern; we are here for you."

As my professor had pointed out, self-disclosure cannot, under any circumstances, be for yourself. That's not to say therapists don't make that mistake. But the ones who are self-aware rein it in as quickly as possible so they can do their jobs.

"You all right?" she asked.

"Yes," I said. "I'm better, thank you for asking. You okay to continue?"

"Sometimes I think I'm getting pretty good at all of this talking stuff," she said. "I can continue."

"Good," I said, with a smile that was somewhat forced due to the mental residue of my self-disclosure. "Tell me more about the anger."

"It's not supposed to be like this," she said. "I'm supposed to come home from work and he's supposed to be there. Now I come home and the house is empty. I'm angry that my life was taken away from me. I'm angry at the doctors who couldn't help him, the whole field of medicine that couldn't treat him. I'm mad at my friends for not having to go through this."

"Who else? Who else are you angry with?"

"I'm angry at God. I've never felt anger toward God before, but I do now. I go to church and I pray and I say the words I'm supposed to say, but as I say them I feel a rage toward Him, toward his Intelligent Design and this 'bereavement' I have to experience so people can create more people. I try to push that feeling away but I know it's there."

"It's okay. This is just like we talked about. Don't push it away. Feel it. Let the feelings come."

"It's just so hard!" Sara said, bursting into tears, a completely new behavior, and a stark change from the smiling woman who had been sitting before me a moment ago. Big, heavy sobs came pouring out as she put her face into her hands. A moment ago she had actually been nurturing me, and now suddenly she was back into her own pain.

She composed herself after a few minutes and her formality returned. "I'm sorry," she said. "This is . . . new to me."

"It is. And you're doing great."

She laughed as she looked at the mascara now covering her hands. "I am? This is what getting better looks like?"

"Strangely, I think it is." *Stay with me, keep going, this will work.*

"Sometimes it's easy to disagree with you, but saying what is in my heart does help."

As the weeks went on, Sara continued to show signs of feeling better. We both could clearly see a pattern where the "bad" days were becoming less frequent and more tolerable. One could say that this was simply a result of "time healing all wounds," and no one could definitively dispute that. But Sara believed that the structure and guidance of therapy was helping to facilitate a change for her.

I asked how she felt about feeling better. "Sometimes I feel guilty," she said. "It's like, if I let the pain go I'm betraying him, being disloyal."

"I don't know if this will help you, but many people say that. You've given your whole adult life to him up to this point. Would it be fair to ask you not to have at least some doubt about feeling better?"

"No, no I suppose not," she said. "In my head I know Mike wants me to be happy, to 'move on,' as they call it. I just need to remind myself of that from time to time."

"How about this? Get an index card to keep in your purse at all times. Write on it, *What would Mike want for me?* If you have any doubts about feeling even an ounce of happiness, take out the card and absorb the words. You mention 'moving on.' What does that mean to you?"

"You mean, other than the filing cabinet analogy?"

"Right. What does it mean to you, specifically?"

"It just means that I won't think about him all the time. I'll sleep like I used to, do things with my friends, and be able to concentrate at work. I won't be angry at God anymore. I want some *control* again."

"Are any of those things happening now?"

She thought for a moment. "Yes, most of those things are."

"Do you think we're almost done with our work together?"

"Soon."

Nine months from the day we met, we began our last sessions. We used them to compose a letter from Sara to Mike. While I worked as her stenographer, she said to him what she called a "so long for now" note. As a homework assignment she would read it over, edit it, add to it, and make it say exactly what she needed to say. When she was finished, she brought the letter into the office and read it aloud to him. This technique is sometimes referred to as the "empty chair" technique, where a person will speak to another as if he were there. The goal again is to simply help facilitate the processing and closure of various thoughts and emotions. This is an approximation of her letter:

Michael,

It's hard for me to go back in my mind to a time where you weren't the most important person in my life. We gave each other everything we had to give. We laughed and cried together; you were my best friend. We didn't have children and our jobs were never what defined us. We lived for each other. When you left, I hated your illness, hated the doctors who couldn't help you, hated God for taking you, and hated you for leaving me here, alone. I couldn't stop crying, no matter where I was or what I was doing. Part of me didn't want that to stop, because if it did, I thought it would mean that I didn't love you anymore. I know that's not true now, but for the longest time I thought I would be betraying you if I started to feel better. I came to see a therapist because I just couldn't handle the pain anymore, and I felt shame in doing so. But I just simply couldn't do it alone. I learned about grief here, about all the feelings that I have a right to have. And that somehow makes me feel better.

Michael, I know now that I have a life worth living without you, at least temporarily, until we're together again. I didn't see that at first, didn't want to see it, but it's true, and I feel better. I'll never, ever stop missing you or loving you, but I need to say good-bye for a little while. I know you won't hate me for that; you always wanted me to have what I wanted, and I want to have some happiness again.

I'll be seeing you again, eventually. Not yet, though. I have more things to do here. I have friends, hobbies. I'm not finished here. I'm still going to come visit you at the cemetery, but not as much, and I won't cry every time I'm there. It's time to let go a bit. For a little while. I miss you, I love you, and when I get to you, we'll pick up where we left off, I promise. I have to go, for now.

Love,
Sara

Pride poured through me. For my teachers, for showing me how to lead someone through such a dark time. For myself, for remembering their words, and for having faith in the process even when Sara was skeptical. And, of course, for Sara. She could have simply given up, become a suicide statistic, or simply a person who moved through every day like a ghost. She could have become like my parents, people who in many ways simply existed. She ultimately picked living over merely existing.

"How does it feel to read that letter to Mike?"

"I feel . . . stronger. I know it won't be like this every day, but right now it feels good."

"I have a feeling you and I are done here."

"Yes," she said. "You know, part of me is going to miss coming here."

"I'll miss that too. I'm very proud of you."

"I'm proud too," she said.

"Are you going to continue to wear your wedding band?"

"Yes, absolutely. I'm still Mike's bride."

"I understand," I said with a smile.

"If I need you, I know where to find you," Sara said. "My filing cabinet is closed for now. I don't need to smash the ball with the paddle. It can just rest."

We stood up and I extended my hand. She took it and put her other hand on top of mine. I could see the wedding band, the symbol of what would be a never-ending cascade of love and commitment from two people.

I thought about how different the therapeutic experience can be with each client. Treatment with Jack was a success in many ways. I helped him grow up, become a young man. He had problems, yes, but at times, he wasn't even aware what those difficulties were. He wasn't "broken," not in the traditional sense.

I thought about David and his OCD, so different from Jack. He knew his problems, yet nothing changed. He didn't improve, let alone grow—at least, not in the way a psychologist would have liked. His treatment was almost a unilateral failure, and he remained broken.

Sara was special to me because she encompassed parts of both Jack and David. She was simply a shell of a person upon starting her treatment. If we could have put a dipstick into her mind and pulled out an objective level of misery, it probably would have matched that of David. But, like Jack, she improved, she grew; she became a new woman in so many ways.

To be part of helping someone who was completely broken heal herself makes everything leading up to it worthwhile. The years of schooling, the countless books read, every test taken, every embarrassing thing you've said in the therapy room, every person you tried to help but couldn't, the drinking and the antidepressants to cope with unrequited love or panic attacks or nailing chairs to the floor, the years of surrounding yourself with people who grapple to find a moment of happiness—it's all worth it.

But I don't have the luxury of basking in the glow of success. Another person needs help, and this time it's me. Now, instead of listening as closely as possible to everything each person has said to me today, I'm suddenly the one doing the talking. I've dropped everyone else's problems to focus on my own.

3 p.m.
The Ghost of Janet

My own therapy wasn't significantly different from the work I did with Sara, given that I had experienced a loss as well. I talked extensively about my thoughts and feelings. My therapist, Carol, would often just listen as I poured on about how foolish I was to think I could get Janet to love me the way I wanted her to. And the talking helped. Along with the Zoloft, over the months I began to feel at least a tinge of happiness.

Carol didn't seem to mind simply being a good listener. Always professionally dressed, she had many of the stereotypical mannerisms of the shrinks that you see depicted in films and on television: She sometimes stroked her chin, said things like "I see," and "How do you feel about that?," and would sometimes blow on her tiny eyeglasses, then clean them with a handkerchief before speaking obscure, cryptic words of wisdom with a confidence that they would help me at some point. "Emotional attachment is a complex being, Rob. If it's not treated as such, it can be all-consuming, leading to both complex grief and depression."

Carol was big on pseudo free-associating. In other words, she encouraged me to simply say whatever came to mind about Janet and the relationship that I never really had, yet had still somehow lost. Although many therapists see catharsis as an overrated exercise, it still has its place and can be of benefit. Sometimes my thoughts were simple:

I miss Janet.
Why didn't she want to be with me?
What did I do wrong to not get her love?
How did I get so attached, so quickly, to someone I didn't even really know?

Simply spewing forth those thoughts helped to dissolve their potency. At other times I had completely irrational cognitions:

She was perfect.
I'll never meet anyone else.
I'm a worthless person and I don't deserve anyone.
I'm nothing without her.

As I said these words aloud and looked at Carol's skeptical eyes and raised brow, I realized they made no sense. And the more I embraced how baseless they were, the thoughts began to disappear from my mind-set altogether.

Carol would periodically ask questions to help clarify certain points about myself that I needed to acknowledge.

"Could you tell me what, exactly, you miss about Janet?"

Today I ask this question to most of my clients who are struggling with loss, but I hadn't thought about it for myself until Carol asked. I didn't have an immediate answer.

"I miss being able to talk to her. We had good conversations. I miss going out on dates with her. She was fun to be with."

"What else?"

"I miss being sexual with her. It was also nice having someone around to hang out with. I felt good with her."

"I'm a little surprised," Carol said. "Those are all things to miss in a person. But you're not describing anything very specific about *Janet*, the 'one and only,' rather, just a person who is worth being with. Are you suggesting that you can't get that from someone else?"

I thought about it as Carol looked at me with her cheerleader's eyes. *Stick with this idea, Rob. I'm going somewhere with this.*

"I'm not sure," I said.

"Think more. What do you miss, specifically, about Janet herself?"

Janet was very good-looking, and at that point in my life, physical attractiveness was an attribute that was more important to me than I liked to admit. She turned heads in bars and restaurants, which made me feel important and envied. *All these guys want to be me.* Our conversations and dates were fun, no doubt about that, but they weren't anything I hadn't shared with another person before. But when I was with this incredibly beautiful and confident woman who made both men and women do double takes, I thought I was the most important person in the world.

"What are you saying?" I asked. "That I don't really miss her per se?"

Carol leaned back in her chair. "You tell me. Could she be more symbolic than real in some ways?"

I paused. "It could be. Janet's looks, her complete security with herself, her blazing confidence, were all turn-ons for me. A life with her meant not only being happy—because I was, in fact, very happy with her—but she was also a status symbol, which meant a lifetime of being the envy of others."

"I wonder, though, if she is a picture of the way you want to feel about yourself as well," Carol said.

This confused me. "It's not that I felt like some inferior, ridiculously insecure person before. My self-esteem was just . . . amped up with Janet. And when she bailed on me, all of the good things about me seemed to disappear as well."

"I'm okay with some of that," said Carol. "Lots of people make us feel things about ourselves that we don't often experience, or at least we experience them to a greater degree. That's partly why we seek out relationships. But, at some level, you seem to be telling yourself that you *need* her to feel great about yourself—that the other things about you don't matter." She paused. "Having heard that, do you really believe such nonsense?"

A slow wave of something rolled over me. Hopefulness?

"No. No, of course not. I don't believe I need her to feel good about myself. It was just *easier* to feel good about myself when I was with her."

"But not in any significant way," she said. "A beautiful woman on your arm ultimately means nothing. Am I correct?"

"Yes. When push comes to shove I placed an undue significance on being envied by others. At least for a reason like that."

Carol leaned forward. "Rob, let me qualify what I'm saying. You have a right to miss her. That in and of itself isn't unhealthy. But you have an obligation to be honest with yourself about *what* you miss, and if that is really coming from her and *only* her, or if it's this mind-game you're playing, telling yourself that you can't be strong and confident on your own, that having some outside validation is really all that important."

Carol's intervention here highlights a specific point in therapy. Some might classify this session as an Aha! moment where the lightbulb goes on and I become a new beacon of mental health. But that wasn't the case here. What Carol did was point out something that, in many ways, I already knew. But it was just ever so slightly out of my grasp. It was just below the surface of my consciousness. I was using Janet to *define* me to the point that I believed every other aspect of myself—my identity as son, friend, psychologist—was irrelevant. It was when Carol took the concept that was just outside of my frame of reference and drove it home that allowed real change to begin.

I didn't immediately become a whole new person based on what she had said, and that new set of feelings she helped to create certainly came and went. But over the next few weeks, as I reminded myself about what she had told me, I started to feel better about myself and less focused on Janet.

Although both the therapy and the Zoloft were helping tremendously, I still had a specific, lingering problem that I couldn't control and that I needed to tackle. Like those who have suffered from trauma, I would often be deluded with thoughts and images that I couldn't push out of my consciousness: I thought a lot about Janet with other men. When we first broke up—to use the phrase loosely, as that implies a real relationship was in place—I would physically see her with other boyfriends. However, our social circles changed over the months, and it got to the point that I would simply occasionally cross paths with her at school. My friends who knew that I was obsessively thinking about her dating other people had told me that she wasn't dating anyone at that moment, and therefore, I didn't have anything to stress about. But still I would simply see flashes in my head, completely out of the blue: in the shower, writing a research paper, doing therapy with my clients. Images of her on a date, being crazy in love with another guy, having sex with him. And no matter what I did I couldn't get the movie in my mind to cease. It was like my brain was fighting against me to create pictures that might not even be occurring.

When I told Carol how jealous I got when I thought about Janet and what I called "my rivals," she had a very specific plan of attack to help me. "What does it feel like, when those images emerge?" she asked.

"It's like I get this anxiety—it just pours over me. My heart starts pounding. It's almost like a mini panic attack. I actually got a little shaky last time, like I couldn't hold a pen to write my name."

"How do you make it stop?"

"At first I was relying on Beer and Tears. Then that stopped helping. It's probably a good thing, because being a drunk probably isn't going to do all that much for my career. So I generally just pace around and try to distract myself. Eventually it goes away, but it just comes back. That depresses me. It depresses me that I get so bent out of shape about not being able to control my own thoughts."

"Who is this person that she is with? A friend? Enemy?"

"That's the thing," I said. "It's no one I know. It's like a phantom person. It's not always even the same person. Lots of times I paint a picture that she's a raging slut who's screwing a new guy every night. Other times it is her soul mate. Both drive me crazy."

At that point Carol decided to teach me an interesting trick.

"You'll get to this in your training at some point, but let's address it here and now. We've talked a lot about how our thoughts influence our mood. People make the assumption, however, that we always think in words. Here is a great example of how your cognitions are actually pictures. The images are your thoughts, which are driving this jealous reaction.

"The good news about this is that images are just like a film, except you are the director. With a little practice you can make the camera do whatever you want. Please, take me through one of these images."

The thought of inducing the very thing that terrified me wasn't what I wanted to do, but since I would be having those thoughts anyway, it made sense to perhaps do something productive with them.

I closed my eyes, hard, and took a deep breath. And then another. "Janet is in her bedroom, lying in bed with a guy. She's gorgeous; she's wearing a negligee that she bought when we were together. She's smiling and being all seductive."

"Now," Carol said, "tell me what this guy looks like."

"He's tall, like six-foot-two, a little bigger than me. He's good-looking. Very good-looking. He's built and strong."

"Is he better-looking than you? Stronger than you?"

"Yes, yes. He's everything I'm not. He's everything she wants and I'm none of that." I gritted my teeth, and through my clenched eyes a tear broke though and worked its way down my cheek. This was the first time in a long while I had cried about Janet. The Zoloft made it hard to in many ways because it helped keep a lot of thoughts at bay. And because I would distract myself when the sex images came into focus, I never tapped into what Carol was now driving at.

"You've created a flawless rival in your head. I'll bet if we extended this description he'd have more money than you, a better personality, funnier, nicer, a better lover. His penis is probably bigger too."

The tear was quickly replaced with a blush. Yes, Mr. Perfect was all of these things. I hated him. Whoever he was.

Carol continued. "The reality is that we don't know who, if anyone, Janet is dating or sleeping with. But it's no wonder these images are taking such a toll on you. Not only are they highly unlikely to be occurring that way, because the scene you describe is more porn than real life, but they also tap into insecurities you have about yourself. And I know, I *know*, you don't really think that badly of yourself."

She was right.

"It's funny," I said. "Janet is always perfect in the image too. In my head I've put her on this pedestal. She always looks gorgeous, never needs makeup or even a shower. I actually dreamt once that she didn't ever use the toilet."

"You've got a vivid imagination," Carol said. "The only problem is that you're using it against yourself instead of in your favor. Let's try something to swing this to your advantage. Where does the movie in your head end?"

The movie never really had an ending because I was always looking for ways to simply stop the projector.

"I don't really know. She marries Mr. Perfect?"

"Close your eyes again," she said, "and take this to the end."

Carol's confidence in the way she gave her directives helped. She often had a look that said *You're going to get through this. I will be there and help you through*, and I always felt safe because of it. I also experienced envy and insecurity; maybe I could never be as good a shrink as she was?

I closed my eyes. "Do I have to go through the whole sex scene? Blow by blow, so to speak? Please don't make me do that."

"If he screws her brains out, which I'm sure he does, and it's mind-boggling, mountain-crumbling sex, because that's how your head works, that's fine. Tell me about after the sex for now and we'll fill in the pieces later."

I mentally DVRed through my self-created pornography. "She's lying in his arms and telling him he's the most incredible thing ever, that she loves him and that she'll be his forever."

Carol actually laughed out loud at this, again, with complete confidence in where she was taking me. "That's ridiculous. You said yourself that she's been cycling through guys all year long. And even if that did happen, you know a lot of young people who have that experience and have it actually *stick?* For the long haul?"

I began to wonder if Carol had her own baggage from years ago. Maybe some bitterness toward young love? That's something I'd probably never find out.

"It's kind of a bleak picture you paint," I said.

"Not exactly," she said. "The reality is that people at that age—or any age, for that matter—can have lots of mindless, awkward sex that culminates in regret the next day. They can also have wild, intense sex that they confuse as love. That's okay; it's normal and natural. It takes years to develop a healthy understanding of one's own sexuality. And yet you've somehow given her this credit that she has everything figured out."

"But how do we know I'm wrong?" I said.

"We don't for sure. But you've bought into this scenario that you've created, 100 percent, lock, stock, and barrel. You took the images as fact. All I'm suggesting is simply an alternative way to consider what might really be happening. I do suspect that Janet is not in this whirlwind of love where she lives happily ever after with

Mr. Perfect, with no problems and no toilets and complete bliss. That's what you're describing."

I relaxed a little bit more. "So what do I do about this?"

"Like most of what we talk about, you need to practice. You need to carry that image through, *realistically*, to the end. Just like everyone else, you stopped the image at the worst part. She orgasms and everything is perfect. Why do you think she is dating a different person so often? Because she doesn't care very much for whomever she's with. Either she wants to be a free spirit, or it's just not working out.

"For example, what happens when you carry the image through and the guy says, 'That was fun . . . I have to go now,' and he takes off, never to call her again? Or when she calls him the next day and says, 'We had a good time, but I don't think I'd like to get too serious'? Or maybe, just maybe, your scene never took place at all?"

It all made sense. "So if I work on changing the images, the way a screenwriter or director would, the pictures won't be so overwhelming."

Carol smiled. "I think that you might get pretty good at doing this for a living someday."

The techniques Carol taught me worked. With some practice I was able to alter the images to create something less than what you'd see in a Nicholas Sparks book or a high-quality skin flick. I made the men she dated a little bit less like Hugh Jackman and remembered that Janet had bodily functions as well. My mind saw her break up with people, get dumped herself, and experience life just like everyone else—as a series of romantic interludes with varying degrees of success and failure. And suddenly the movie wasn't all that intriguing anymore. "When images become boring, they go away. And, fortunately, so do your symptoms," Carol said.

After a few weeks of training my mind, I had a much greater sense of control and peace. Having done six months of the Zoloft/Carol treatment regimen, it began to look like both wouldn't be necessary in my life all that much longer.

4 p.m.
Till Death Do Us Part . . . or Not?

Years after Janet, I was living with a girlfriend, whom I'll call Melissa. We had been together for a little over a year when we decided to move in together. At the time I asked her to move into my apartment with me, she hesitantly agreed, stating, "I don't want to play house; I've done that before. I'd like to be married someday."

"I'd like that, too," I said. "Let's live together for a little while, and if it works out then we'll get engaged."

I was sincere. I wasn't ready to be married just then, but I knew I could make a relationship work. After all, I was a psychologist. If a professional like me with perfect communication skills and an outstanding ability to listen couldn't maintain a solid, healthy relationship, then who could?

After one year of living together things were perfect in most, if not all, of the ways professionals would consider crucial: communication, shared interests, a maintaining of personal identity through individual activities, a healthy sex life. Arguments in an intimate relationship are par for the course; fortunately, ours were limited in frequency and intensity and usually had a productive course and positive resolution. Our friends and family described us as a great couple.

And then something changed. At thirty-one years of age I fancied myself young, successful, and just hitting my professional and personal stride. I wanted to write, see the world, grow my practice to the point that I needed to hire consultants to see the overflow of clients that would invariably want to visit my office. Could I do those things with Melissa in my life? Of course. And yet, why get tied down? We could still continue to live together and see where things went—couldn't we? I began to rationalize my hesitation to Melissa on moving forward.

"Why hold each other back?" I said. "Society says we need to be married, but who knows what each of us will want down the line. Maybe we should keep our options open."

She had every right to be angry for not only breaking my initial promise to her, but then failing to own up to my own fears and self-ishness. "Hold each other back? Is that what being with me means?"

"It's not *you;* it's just that I want to do things in my life."

"I don't stop you!"

"I know, it's just . . . this is scary. It's like, the end of being just . . , me."

She sighed, sat down on our couch, and put her face in her hands. "Of course you don't want to make a greater commitment to me," she said, eyeliner now pulled across her cheeks. "You don't see marriage as a way to grow; you see it as a way to die."

She was right, but I wasn't ready to admit it at the time. Selfish? Afraid? *Me?* I got defensive and accused her of pushing me toward something for which I wasn't ready. Sometimes relationships reach a tipping point, a buildup to an apex where things permanently shift. Here we were.

The arguments began to escalate in frequency and intensity. And although my head clearly was misaligned on marriage and commitment, Melissa was no victim. She would hit below the belt by using harsh language, suddenly starting quarrels about benign things that had never bothered her before ("Can't you remember to put the fucking top back on the toothpaste?!"), all the while not realizing that those behaviors made it that much easier for me to pull away from her. It became a vicious cycle: distancing, fighting, more distancing, more fighting, over and over and over. When I finally said that perhaps we should see a therapist to try to salvage the relationship, I unfortunately knew, perhaps subconsciously, that the odds were stacked against us. Going to couples therapy sometimes actually signals the beginning of the end of a relationship.

Couples therapy has a horrible track record for two reasons: One is that the couple usually waits far too long to seek help, long after arguments have gotten out of hand and the pair has drifted in a negative direction that usually means the relationship can't be saved. Unfortunately, couples often arrive for therapy with some knowledge that the relationship is either hanging by a thread or even that one or both members is seeking a sort of permission to dissolve the connection. I was faced with both. Although the thought of being without Melissa was terrifying—we had logged almost three years together—I wanted out. I wasn't ready for a permanent commitment. And by the time she had yelled herself nearly to death at me, I knew I didn't want anything lifelong with someone who had such a strong temper, even if I was the facilitator of much of the screaming. And by the time that realization had been spoken by me, Melissa had already drawn the same conclusion. We were done.

The other reason that couples work brings home a poor report card is that "therapy success" is often measured by whether or not the couple stays together. When I told a professor of mine that I thought a good therapist could make any couple a happier one, she pointed out that I was being naïve, not only about the notion that "therapy can fix everything" but also my implicit assumption that "every marriage is meant to go the distance."

"Sometimes all you can do is give your blessing to a couple that it's time to move on," she said. "There's no shame in that, and it's your professional obligation to do so." Some might view this as a controversial take on treatment, especially those counselors who view marriage as a sacrament, but the reality is that it is unethical to try to force a square peg into a round hole. If people are truly miserable together, and it's clear that this isn't going to change, regardless of the promises made at one point in time, the shrink's role is to help them to separate and live happier lives apart.

Depending on where you get your numbers, one out of every two new marriages ultimately ends in divorce. Statistics are dubious entities and this number can vary wildly depending on your source (you can find rates as low as 30 percent and as high as 60 percent), but even as a simple approximation, a 50 percent divorce rate is a scary proposition. There is some fluctuation in this number depending on certain demographics: A lower divorce rate is seen in those who are college-educated, as well as those who wait until they are over age thirty before getting married. If you marry in your teens or early twenties, your risk of the relationship dissolving escalates significantly.

What makes this "one in two" figure even more sobering is the reality that the 50 percent of marriages that remain intact are not all, in fact, happy ones. I see both individuals and couples who remain in relationships for a plethora of reasons: financial, religious, a belief that it benefits the children, a perception that one doesn't deserve better, fear of being alone, or simply a lack of desire to deal with the legal red tape. If we look for the number of "successful" marriages that include both a formal marriage license as well as mutual satisfaction, we are considering a fairly low number that hasn't been well established in the clinical literature. Melissa and I never got down the aisle, which, in retrospect, was a good thing. Some might argue that we should never have lived together in the first place, that our possibly casual take on the romantic bond made it too easy to split up. But there's no doubt that had we taken the vows and stuck it out, we would have become one of those couples who simply went through the motions, never thriving as a pair.

There are countless books, seminars, lecture series, workshops, and marriage counselors available to couples. And yet why do so many marriages "fail" in the broad sense of the word? Putting aside obvious precipitating factors such as abuse, addictions, or adultery, the focus here is on some of the most salient reasons why marriage can be such a difficult business:

1. *Marriage requires compatibility not just at the point of saying "I do," but across the entire life span.*

You won't be the same person in five, ten, or twenty years. Your goals, ideals, perspectives, and interests can all change as you evolve. This isn't a bad thing. However, as you move along throughout your adulthood as an ever-changing being, your spouse is doing the same thing. Two people who marry at twenty-five won't be the same people at thirty-five or forty-five, so your compatibility over the life span of the marriage requires that you both evolve in mutually beneficial ways. This is no easy task, and it's why you often hear of couples "growing apart," or of one partner saying "He/she isn't the person I married." Melissa and I were a perfect match during our courtship and first year of living together. Then I changed, which created the perfect opportunity for her to change as well. Couples need to realize that they will both be different people down the road, and thus have to strive for changes that allow them to remain connected in a viable way.

The best way to address this together is to first acknowledge the issue. Couples who are considering marriage should ask themselves and each other: Where could one of us be in a year, three years, thirty years? What are the potential barriers to us "growing old together"? What will we do if one of us drastically strays from our current plan? You don't need to have definite statements, but answers such as "Don't worry, that won't happen" will not suffice. There needs to be an acknowledgment that a real deviation could occur for one or both partners, and that, ideally, it will be discussed and managed together.

Picture your self-growth as a vertical line advancing upward with deviations to the left and right. Those deviations could include a change in job focus, a loss of sexual attraction, a newfound desire to have a child (or perhaps more children), or a new location in which you wish to live. Your partner has a similar line and it will move as well, also forward and left/right. If those lines don't remain at least somewhat parallel to each other over the adult life span, the relationship will become unsatisfying.

2. *Assuming that marriage implies monogamy, the institution itself is counterintuitive to biology.*

Most species, including humans, are not hardwired to be with one individual. You're programmed to be producing with different partners. Almost invariably people report that they often feel a sexual attraction to others who are not their spouse. While many do not act on those drives, people often view this as a sign that "the marriage is not meant to be," or that the relationship is inherently flawed. This usually happens around the time when sexual excitement wanes and it becomes harder to live a passionate lifestyle in the bedroom. This realization of a damaged relationship isn't necessarily accurate simply because our makeup promotes the seeking out of new mates. What most people don't realize is that the ideal marriage means striving for a greater good than can be obtained in lieu of multiple sex partners. But make no mistake: Marriage is a man-made institution, not a natural one. Without an appreciation for the magnitude of commitment prior to starting the marriage, both sexual and emotional, a person can become disenchanted very quickly. This is particularly unfortunate with patients who leave positive relationships due to finding a more sexually desirable partner. For some of these people, they float through dozens of mates, believing that there is that one person who will be able to fulfill every sexual idea, fantasy, and need.

3. *There is far too much emphasis on weddings as opposed to marriages.*

I often ask this to patients who seem hyperfocused on their wedding day: Pretend that I could marry you and your perfect mate (real or imagined) right now. By simply reading this paragraph, you are married. For women this means no ring, friends, family, flowers, dress, undivided attention, or celebration of any kind. For men this means no bachelor party, tuxedo, strippers, or best man. Neither of you would even be signing papers down at City Hall. Just this and you're legally committed. Do you still want to be married to this person right now?

Those who say "no" or hesitate for more than a few seconds before replying are immediately setting themselves up for failure. Don't confuse the terms *wedding* and *marriage*. Your wedding occurs on Day 1, but the marriage is every single day after that. Can you name any other situation where one would devote so much focus on less than .001 percent of the pie? Unfortunately, women (and some men) are taught that the wedding day is the most important thing in a person's life. You don't need to watch reality shows about brides from hell to know how inherently self-absorbed people can become when it comes to their wedding because of the emphasis placed on it. It's a person's fifteen minutes of fame. But the price tag that comes with that fleeting moment of glory can be colossal. Unless you are fully prepared to be with your partner regardless of the means to get there, you're missing the point of the institution.

4. *Many couples do not know how to fight fairly.*

This is somewhat of a cliché in the shrink world but true nonetheless. There are countless books and therapeutic approaches on this topic, but the long and short of it is that any successful long-term relationship will have its fair share of conflict. This is a natural aspect of emotional intimacy. But too many people shy away from raising their voices or asserting their needs to each other for multiple reasons: fear of abandonment, a belief that fighting is a sign that the relationship is failing, an inherent desire to not be like other couples who are constantly screaming at each other, etc. At the other extreme, there are couples who simply can't control their emotions, where every day brings a new, explosive battle in the relationship. And of course there are always relationships where one partner is a fighter and the other a peacekeeper. This was the dynamic that Melissa and I developed. Her anger led her to pick verbal altercations with me that had no place in the relationship. And because I knew where this anger was coming from, my knee-jerk reaction was to attempt to put the fire out. My guilt didn't allow me to assert myself, which simply validated and reinforced her anger.

Fair, balanced fighting is an art that many couples simply can't master. It involves a mutual respect for both your own and your partner's emotional state, a verbal working through of the feelings and issues, and a resolution. No shrink would promote verbal or physical abuse in a relationship, but those worth their salt know that anger and its expression are part of the human condition and shouldn't always be suppressed. This is because over a long period of time, resentment and a lack of fulfillment result.

One technique that helps couples was taught to me by a supervisor in graduate school. She called it the mirror trick: Before you approach your partner with a grievance, take a mental peek into the mirror. What aspect of yourself, what issues or "stuff," either past or present, are you bringing to the discussion about this problem? For example, if you don't like the amount of time your partner spends with friends, ask yourself "What does his/her spending time away from me mean to me specifically?" It could be an issue of feeling inferior to them or unwanted, something that cuts beyond the core of "A man/woman needs to be home with his/her spouse." If you can "look in the mirror" first you can then approach your partner with the grievance in the form of your personal idiosyncrasy with the issue as opposed to simply pointing the finger. This will often decrease defensiveness and lead to a more-productive outcome. Consider: "When you spend such a large amount of time with your friends, it taps into my fears that you don't want to be with me. I feel inferior to them." Compare this with: "I hate it when you're with your friends so much. You need to be home more." Which approach is more likely to get the more-productive response?

There is a little-known secret in the mental health world: Many couples that don't ever fight eventually don't have sex either. Why? They are both forms of passion. If you give up one form of intensity, you'll ultimately leave the other as well. It may take many years, but couples have reported this problem to me time and time again.

5. *Marriage doesn't solve problems.*

Unfortunately, marriage often amplifies problems. The number of times individuals and couples in the office have said "Once we got married I assumed he would stop putting me down," or "After the wedding day I assumed she would want to have sex more often" is mind-boggling. A ring or a marriage certificate doesn't improve an individual's insecurities, solve problems, or alter personalities. The increase in physical proximity and time spent together will likely increase any issues already present.

The fact that one has problems isn't a reason to not get married; rather, it's a sign to start to address those difficulties and not assume they will "take care of themselves." Had Melissa and I gone forward and gotten married, it's unlikely her anger and resentment would have subsided, because she knew that I would have been going through with it simply for *her*, not for me or for us.

6. *People settle for less than what they want.*

Society puts a colossal pressure on people, especially women, to be married. If a woman doesn't have a partner, many people wonder what's wrong with her. Some of this thought process is natural, as humans are social creatures and we have a natural tendency to come together with another. But many people who enter their thirties or beyond without having been married are perceived as flawed, or at least weird. Because of society's demands, many make a decision to get married based on poor reasoning: to have children, to not be alone, to find someone who fits an arbitrary mold, or to satisfy their parents' and society's demands. If one is making a lifelong decision to meet ulterior motives, it's not likely to bring much happiness.

7. *Couples assume they are immune to reasons one through six, and believe that hard work isn't part of the deal. They think that love, sex, children, or some combination thereof will be enough.*

Some research suggests that only 10 percent of couples maintain the intense "puppy love" experience years into their partnership. Whether or not that bliss can sustain a marriage in and of itself is up for debate, but the reality is that for most couples, no force other than mutual effort can power a relationship. And if you refuse to buy into the idea that marriage is work, that your feelings will simply carry you through, you'll ultimately be disappointed. A partnership of such intensity requires a commitment to building and nurturing it. It's not unlike your physical body: Without a decent diet, exercise, and various healthy lifestyle choices (e.g., not smoking, drinking alcohol only in moderation), you will decay at a rate much faster than nature might want. Marriage requires maintenance and effort as well, or else it will collapse. I've had couples say to me, "That's so unromantic. It shouldn't be work; we should be able to do this naturally if we truly love each other." While I wish I could agree with them on that score, it's simply not reality, and this viewpoint is the precipitator for so many of the marital problems seen today.

Fortunately, many couples do make their relationship work, and they lead mutually satisfying lives together. And while it is rare that two people see a therapist to simply enhance their already-solid relationship (treatment here is sometimes based on what is called a "growth model"), couples that are struggling can benefit from therapy. One anonymous psychiatrist pointed out that if my reasons for why romantic relationships fail is accurate, then therapy could help by "reorienting disoriented people's expectations about their marriage, or, perhaps people should go into counseling before they get married in the first place."

What makes couples work so compelling is that treatment goals vary so starkly. When an individual begins therapy for depression, an obvious goal is to improve his mood. When he presents with a phobia, the focus is to decrease anxiety around the feared object. But with couples the problems cut across so many stripes of difficulties. Some couples need help with their sex lives; others argue too much or unproductively; some are dealing with an extramarital affair and are hoping to continue the relationship; and yet others don't know how to balance their lives as both partners and parents. However, when the presenting problems are discussed further, when all of the theories of couples work are considered, when problems are boiled down to their basic elements, successful treatment usually centers around understanding both one's own communication style and that of his/her partner's, as well as making those two styles mesh together.

When couples' relationships have improved through our work together, they often are able to remember a key principle in communication: content versus process. *Content* refers to the actual topic or specifically spoken words. *Process,* on the other hand, is the way the topics and words play out: the deeper meanings, the *way* words are spoken, the overarching messages sent (this is sometimes known as *meta*-communication). Couples rarely make headway when they focus solely on the content of their communication, but tend to have fuller, more comprehensive relationships when they focus on process.

Consider my work with a couple in their mid-thirties, whom I'll call Jeff and Sandra. For the most part they were a relatively happy couple with successful careers in business, and one child. They had been married for about three years and had dated for two years prior to taking their vows.

Jeff and Sandra, however, would engage in unproductive arguments. Jeff would often perceive his wife as not understanding him, and she would view him as unable to be placated. Somewhat opposite of what gender stereotypes would suggest, yet they were both correct.

When Jeff would recount examples of the exchanges with Sandra, it quickly became apparent what was wrong. "When she wasn't home within an hour of when she said she would be, I got upset."

"He always does this," said Sandra. "He's always 'upset' because I spend time with friends outside of work and don't always get home when I say I will."

"She apologizes for being late, which I can accept, but I keep pushing her not to do it again."

"I get annoyed because I say it ultimately wasn't a big deal; I never know what to say to help calm him down."

"Let's go back to one of the first things you said," I interjected. "What does that term mean, 'upset'?"

"I don't know if I understand what you're asking."

"The word 'upset' is kind of a basket term for emotions. It doesn't really tell us anything other than something doesn't feel right. It's like 'uncomfortable' or 'distressed.' We use them socially without a problem, but they are basically empty words. They don't describe what you were feeling when she didn't come home. Sandra, do you get what I mean?"

"Yes, absolutely. I'm not entirely sure what that means either, other than that something is wrong."

"Right," I said. "Your styles of communication are not gelling, and you're focusing solely on one topic: Sandra's desire to spend time with friends and periodically forgetting to call home when she is running late. But there's more here."

"So if I didn't feel upset, what did I feel?" Jeff asked.

"Well, only you would know that for sure, but many options come to mind. If you perceived her lateness as a sign of disrespect, you might feel angry. If you thought she might be late because she was with another man, you might feel jealous. If you thought that maybe she was hurt or in danger, you could feel anxious. I'm sure there are probably many more possibilities as well."

"I think I felt anxious."

"That's a good start. How did you decide that? You thought she was hurt, like in a car accident or something?"

"No, I thought she might leave me."

"Why would she leave you?" I asked.

"Rationally, I don't think she would. But years ago when the relationship was still young, we had a huge fight and she threatened to break up with me. She didn't call me for a few days, and I had no idea where she was, or what our status was; I felt completely lost and afraid."

"So when she didn't come home it reminded you of that time, when you thought you might lose her? Was the feeling then the same as now?"

"Absolutely."

"Sandra, what do you think of this?" I asked.

"I had no idea he felt those things," she said in an empathic tone. "I'm not leaving you, Jeff."

"Now you two are getting somewhere. This wasn't just some vague emotional freak-out. At some level you were afraid she had left, that she was gone. Now we're talking about *process*, the undercurrent of the dialogue you two have when discussing this. This isn't about who is where at what time, and who should be calling who; that's just the content. This is about abandonment and reassurance, and understanding deeper meanings behind what you experience in the day-to-day operations of being a couple. This will help both of you because you, Jeff, will feel more understood, and you, Sandra, will have a better understanding of what is rattling Jeff's cage. That will help guide each of your behaviors."

It might sound overly simplistic to say that this couple's marriage improved via one concept, but it's true nonetheless. Now one could argue that Jeff could stand to be less "needy" and more confident in the relationship, and that his wife should be more socially conscientious, and usually those issues get discussed at some point in the treatment. But as an initial point of intervention, it falls flat, as this line of discourse is exactly what got Jeff and Sandra into trouble in the first place. They placed content over process.

Given that marriages so often do not work out even though there are ways to improve upon them and make them satisfying, what message about committed relationships should people take from this? It's actually quite simple: If you decide to commit to a single person for the rest of your life, know that the road can be a long and difficult one. It may not work out, possibly through no one's fault. By that I mean that you might not be happy with this person throughout the course of your life for any number of reasons. But if you recognize these potential pitfalls, commit to the work involved, and seek out help before the relationship is hanging by a thread, you will significantly increase your chances of a healthy relationship. That is all that anyone can ask for.

5 p.m.
The Root of All Evil?

Years ago, I got a call from my friend Dan in New York City. "Fuck them!" he screamed into the phone. "This is bullshit! I work my ass off for them, and this is all I get?!"

I was doing my postdoctoral studies at an inpatient facility in upstate New York at the time, a one-year apprenticeship commonly tackled after psychologists-to-be have received their doctorates but haven't yet obtained the requisite hours for licensure. In other words, you can call yourself "Dr. So-and-So," but you don't have permission to practice independently. Therefore, you work for a hospital or clinic until you've gained two thousand hours of additional training; then you can go out on your own. This is analogous to what physicians go through after they complete medical school.

"Fuck who?"

"The partners!"

Dan was in his fourth year at a prestigious law firm in midtown Manhattan, working his way up the corporate ladder as a cracker-jack attorney. At this point in time, I had already done six full years of academic training, while he was able to get a great job after only six semesters of law school. His salary was almost ten times what I was making, which was a moot point, given that Dan was born into money and only entered law for what he perceived would be the intellectual challenge of the work. My $25,000+ per annum was less than most managers make at local fast-food chains. But because Dan was a bizarrely hard worker who would easily clock eighty hours per week in a fast-paced and high-pressure environment, I would try to give him empathy about his job whenever possible.

"So what did they do this time?" I asked.

"Twenty-six thousand—that's it!"

"Twenty-six thousand what, exactly?"

"Dollars. That's all I got for my year-end bonus."

Earlier that day, I had worked with a woman who had been diagnosed with paranoid schizophrenia. After two months in the hospital, she had made enough progress to finally go home. We spent our last session together helping her maximize her food stamps that were waiting for her when she got back to her one-room apartment. To this day, I don't think I have met someone as thankful as she was for having someone take the time to help her make the most of what little she had. She truly knew the importance of appreciating what you have, very much *un*like the person on the other end of the line. As Dan breathed heavily into the phone from near hyperventilation induced by his fury, one of the secretaries handed me a card and a box. It was from the president of the hospital:

> *Dear Dr. Dumbrewsky:*
>
> *To say that your work here is appreciated would be an understatement. Please accept this gift (a "year-end bonus," if you will) from the Board of Trustees, as a token of what your contributions mean to us.*

I opened up the box and found a dark blue sweatshirt with the hospital emblem emblazoned on the left sleeve, and a twenty-dollar bill poking out of the pocket. As Dan continued to rant about the current injustices being foisted upon him, I held up the shirt, then the twenty. Two thoughts began to emerge: 1) Unless I change my name to Dr. Ruth or Dr. Phil, I'll never be wealthy in this business; and 2) Greed is a psychological phenomenon for which I'll never develop a true tolerance, even in close friends.

Click.

Graduate school teaches psychologists-in-training very little, if anything, about the financial aspects of working in the mental health field. Many university professors do not practice privately and often have only a cursory knowledge of the interface between being a practitioner and a businessperson. During my training in the late 1990s, my school offered a reduced-fee clinic for the community that was based on personal income. Patients paid as little as $2 per session, and it was almost unheard-of for anyone to pay more than $25, regardless of how much money the person had. Discussing finances rarely, if ever, became part of the treatment process, except under unusual circumstances when a client couldn't afford anything at all. Many of the professors believed that everyone receiving services should be required to pay something if they were going to be seen in our clinic regularly. "Even if it's just one dollar, it's a symbolic gesture," one supervisor pointed out. "It's a way of saying 'Thank you for trying to help me.' "

"And what, exactly, are we going to do with such impressive fees?" my future colleague John asked. "Three sheets of paper for the copy machine? A new pencil? One Rorschach card?"

John had always planned to run a very upscale, "boutique" private practice in New York City, and everyone in school knew this. Thus his remarks about finances were never treated with much gravitas. His goal was to help as many destitute people as possible during his training and then cash in after getting his license by charging exorbitant prices as a child psychologist. This early charity work would help stave off any Catholic guilt he anticipated experiencing later. He ultimately was successful on all counts.

"You know what the best part of being a doctor will be, Dobrenski?" John whispered.

"We aren't going to be real doctors," I said.

"Your name is going to be *Doctor* Dobrenski, is it not?"

"Yes, but . . ."

"All right, then, so shut up. My point is that the best part will be the 'doctor's note.' You can get people out of anything by just saying so. *That's* power."

"If I had a doctor's note from you right now, I could get out of this lecture about how we need to collect at least four quarters from every patient," I said.

"Exactly. What do you want the first doctor's note you write to look like?" John asked.

I thought about this for a few minutes and came up with the following:

Dear non-doctor:

Please excuse Mr. X (a non-doctor, not unlike yourself) from work during the hours of 1–2:30 p.m. today, as he has an appointment, a doctor's appointment no less, with me, the doctor. I will be performing doctor-related procedures with him, things that you could not possibly understand, being that you are not a doctor yourself. Should you become a doctor (like me), please feel free to let me know.

Sincerely,

DOCTOR Rob Dobrenski

"How about you?" I asked.

John looked at mine. "Damn, I was just going to say, 'Let so-and-so out of work because I say so and am charging him $250 per hour. If you have a problem with that, go fuck yourself.'"

"Both work," I said. "But do you think people will respond well to psychologists who curse a lot?"

"What do I care?" John said. "Lots of people curse. If people want to stick their heads in the sand and believe that their shrink or obstetrician or brain surgeon isn't a regular schmo, that's their fucking problem."

What made John such an interesting person was his lust for being alive. Did he want to make a truckload of money in psychology? Absolutely. But he simply *loved* life and wanted to teach others how to do that as well. That was his calling. He worked from a model I called "Psychologist First, Businessman Second."

During our last year of graduate school John and I took part in a research protocol about first impressions. The study involved a group of undergraduate students who rated each other on dozens of personality variables (e.g., likability, gregariousness, introversion, etc.) at an initial group meeting. Then the students would spend weeks and weeks together, kind of like some academic reality show, only to rate their peers again on the same variables at the end of the study.

Because John and I were so far along in our graduate training, we were considered experts in personality. Our job was to watch hours of videotape showing the students interacting together, both in group settings and in one-on-one dialogues. Based on what we watched, we rated the students on the same personality variables. Comparing the students' initial takes on each other with both their later ratings, as well as the "experts'" opinions, would ideally shed some light on how accurate first impressions are.

John and I got together a few times per week in a small room (the "lab") on the top floor of our university's main building. We were actually in a tower and I would often suggest that John let his long, blond hair flow out the window like Rapunzel did. He never found it all that funny.

When we watched the tapes I put on a white lab coat that I had found in the closet. "You a real scientist now, Dobrenski?" John asked.

"I like to take my work seriously."

"Me, too. Hand me that six-pack of Corona."

We watched hours and hours of tape of these ten or so students hanging out together. Even as they got to know one another, however, they all seemed pretty reserved and reticent. John hated that.

"These people are so fucking *boring*," he said, slicing up a lime to go into his beer. He actually brought a cutting board to the lab.

"Maybe it gets more intimate when they do the one-on-ones."

"I hope so. Some of the chicks aren't all that bad."

The one-on-ones were not, in fact, more intimate. Most of the guys tried to act like perfect gentlemen when talking to the ladies, and the women presented themselves as demure and straitlaced.

"Maybe being filmed makes it hard for them to let their hair down," I said. "Speaking of which, why don't you . . ."

"Will you please shut the fuck up about my hair and this god-damned tower?"

Each person in the study had pre-scripted questions to ask during the one-on-ones. During one session a woman referred to her card and then asked the man sitting across from her, "What would be the most absolutely perfect day for you?"

The guy thought about it for what seemed like forever. "Well, I think I'd like to get up at a pretty early hour and go for a long run. Then I'd come home and take a hot shower, followed by a great breakfast with my friends. Then we'd go kayaking for the afternoon. I'd come home and call my girlfriend and we'd go out for a nice dinner and maybe a movie."

"That's nice," the woman said.

"Sounds like kind of a standard Sunday to me," I said.

"What the fuck?" John said. "This is such bullshit. The guy has no clue how to live. A college kid, in his stupid Abercrombie and Fitch hat and popped-collar polo shirt, thinks his *perfect* day involves rowing a boat and eating dinner? Where's the money? The chicks? The blunts?"

"He's probably just holding out to not look stupid."

"No way; this guy just doesn't get it. She asked about his 'absolutely perfect' day. Not a good day, not a great day, not one of the best days, but his *perfect* day. This guy doesn't know shit about mental health. You can't even put a price on the cost of the lessons he needs to learn. How many lives does this idiot thinks he gets to live?"

"What would your perfect day be?" I asked.

John paused for a moment. "My perfect day would begin with a big, fat blow job from that nursing student who won't give me the time of day."

"I see. A regular blow job won't cut it? It has to be big and fat?"

"Right. Then a masseuse would show up and work on me for about an hour, followed by some time in the sauna. If it was a Sunday in the fall, by early afternoon I'd be on the fifty-yard line for the most important football game of the year, drinking beer and talking with Steven Spielberg."

"He likes football?" I asked.

"I don't know. Who cares? It's my perfect day and he's my favorite director. So I'd catch an errantly thrown ball, which Steve would sign, and after the game he, Deion Sanders, and I would hit the best restaurant in whatever city we were in. Then I'd get a call from Pamela—"

"Anderson?"

"Right. She'd call to ask me to go to over to Hef's place for a small party with the bunnies. I'd have sex with all of them—"

"How many women would that involve?"

"Umm . . . nine."

"All at once, like a ten-some, or separate experiences?"

"Both."

"Fascinating."

"Then Hugh would hit me up with a few C-notes for being so cool and I'd take a limo back to Pam's place. She'd ask me to marry her that night, and, although I'd decline because of my newfound status as a sex machine, I'd put her in my Rolodex for future encounters. She'd be perfectly happy with that."

"I'm glad you're so thoughtful toward her needs as well."

"Damn straight," he said, and threw back the last of his beer.

I knew from the day I met John that he was hard-core on many levels. But at twenty-seven years old, having had been nothing but a student my whole life, I hadn't *lived* all that much. At least not the way John did, or how his fantasies suggested he wanted to live. Right then I wanted to be like him. Not because he was drinking beer during a research study or pissing on a student for having such a lame fantasy or because of the Playboy bunnies, but because of his brazen love of life.

While John makes a small fortune as a practicing psychologist, the money is merely an added benefit of his passion for the field and his goal of creating a high quality of life for everyone who walks through his office door. He wants to be the best at his job while making a nice living doing so. For those reasons John deserves the income he gets.

There is another way to run a practice, which is essentially the antithesis of John's: Businessman First, Psychologist Second. This is the model that my colleague, Dr. Steve, employs. Like John, Steve enjoys making money, and he's very good at doing just that. In fact, he makes significantly more than John; although neither were willing to share their income-tax returns with me, I'm approximating that in 2008, Steve took in about $350K to John's $225K. But psychology is simply a means to an end for Steve. He just wants as much cash to line his pockets as is humanly possible. He doesn't care all that much about the job, and is often disappointed when clients improve. "Why wouldn't I be upset? It's a loss of income."

His greed is only surpassed by the psychological tactic he employs to get more clients: charge as much as possible knowing that many people will erroneously believe that "you get what you pay for." He tells them about his Ivy League education and many years' experience, meaning that, therefore, he is "the best."

My postdoctoral training was at an Ivy League hospital. While outstanding in its own way, it wasn't really any better than the tiny community mental health center in a small, midwestern town where I trained as a graduate student. Indeed, although the Ivy League hospital may have featured psychologists and psychiatrists in nicer suits and bigger offices, people with psychological problems don't necessarily get better care simply because they walk into Harvard as opposed to Joe's Mental Health Clinic. And while this might be construed as an overly simplistic view, many clients have been duped into believing it by people like Steve.

The human condition is so complex and constantly evolving, and no one person or institution has all the answers. Therapy will never be an exact science, and therefore there will never be the perfect textbook or teacher or school that will create the Ultimate Therapist who puts his hand on your head and cures you of any and every ill. But Steve knows that many people are unaware of these facts. His wealthy clients will believe that he's worth it because he's so expensive. They'll tell their other rich friends that he's a status symbol in many ways because of his price tag, and if they can afford it, then good for them. But the reality is that Altoids don't taste any better if you pay $59 for the tin.

I learned a lot about Steve during a brief period where we worked out at the same gym. Steve is about ten years older than me—although in much better shape—and occasionally we would see each other in the locker room where we'd shoot the breeze about how our practices were faring.

On one particular day, post-handball, Steve revealed to me that he'd recently had a very successful session during which he had convinced a man not to commit suicide. He wouldn't go into many details with me about the session, as he likes to remain mysterious when it comes to his interventions. Steve was, however, more than happy to share with me the argument that ensued between him and the client after the session.

"He was so sure that he was going to off himself before the session started, but then I worked my magic," Steve said in his usual offhand way, as if he has saved thousands from suicide over the years. He picked up his Rolex and cufflinks and then rubbed pomade through his salt-and-pepper hair.

"What kind of magic?" I asked.

"You know, consequences—family will miss you—can't take it back once you've done it—whatever. When the session was over and I asked him to pay his bill, he was all incredulous: 'I can't believe you'd ask for money after this!' "

"What did you say?"

"I said, 'Why wouldn't I? I expect to be paid for my services. So let's get to it.' "

Kinder words have never been spoken. "So what happened?" I asked.

"Oh, he paid the fee, but he left in a bit of a huff, so I'm not sure he'll be back. I saved that fucker's life and this is the thanks I get."

Strangely, I agreed with Steve in a certain way. When a client sees that death isn't the only option available to him, when he's thinking more clearly, when he is feeling better, he is often so grateful that a unique bond is formed. However, it's important to recognize that this bond, for better or worse, is predicated on the fact that helping this person is what psychologists do for a living. It's how the bills get paid. It is, in fact, a business. So, at the end of the day, even though Steve had talked a man down from the ledge, he still wanted the money he had worked for—and in many ways, he had earned it more during that session than any other.

The problem isn't the money. The problem is that Steve *only* deals in money. He doesn't care about the job, about helping others. Psychology is simply a conduit to a life of material goods for Steve. He states—quite often, actually—that he doesn't have a passion or even an active liking for his work or the people he treats. It's simply a source of income. So, although both John and Steve are successful psychologists who are good at what they do, they are completely different people. And while I do not know how many Dr. Steves there are in the world today, make no mistake: They do exist. When you walk through their office doors, look closely at their eyeballs; the dollar signs are there.

The interface of psychology and business doesn't generate issues solely on the practitioner's end. Clients themselves have their share of problems when the concept of the Almighty Dollar is brought up. Many psychologists, especially in large, urban areas, do not accept private insurance, so clients often are required to pay "out of pocket." Many are hesitant to do so, however. They might haggle or even attempt to barter for services. Some clinicians see these actions as a discredit to the service, and have a singular price that is not to be negotiated. Others utilize what is known as a "sliding scale," where the fee is based on reported income. (Note: Some therapists will work on an honor system in this regard, while others will insist on viewing a tax return to verify income.)

There are times when people will present with unusual or very problematic financial situations. For example, when I received a call from the wife of a middle-aged couple that was seeking treatment, and was claiming to be in dire straits for money, I considered their difficulties:

"We'd love to make an appointment, Doctor, but the truth is that my husband Ted doesn't make much money. He's in retail, and I'm not working at the moment," she said.

"Well, the normal fee is $160 per session, but I can slide that down to $125 for you if that will help you get treatment."

"Is there anything else you can do, anything at all? Our last therapist only charged us $75."

"I'm sorry, my policy is to offer people a reduced rate that is no lower than $125 per session. I hope you understand."

"Doctor, I'm really at a loss here on where to go. Our last therapist retired, and no one on our insurance plan can see us for at least one month. We will work very, very hard in therapy. Our marriage is so conflicted right now. Maybe you could see us for $100 per session?"

The woman, whom I'll call Amy, sounded both very desperate and very sincere, and stated that her husband, "Ted," was equally distressed.

What I ultimately offered her was a temporary fee of $100 with an agreement that we would adjust to the normal amount when she began working. She was more than happy to work with this fee structure.

"Oh, yes, yes! I work in film, so it is a little touch and go, you know, in terms of money coming in, but I will promise to keep you posted."

Amy, Ted, and I started working together a few days later, and it was intense right from the get-go. Well-dressed and professional-looking, within minutes they bombarded me with problems more likely to be seen on *Jerry Springer* than in a therapist's office. Both parties had recently had affairs, there was one incident of domestic violence—he had slapped her across the face, and when he turned to walk away she returned the favor by shoving him down the steps, breaking his collarbone—and Ted's mother had recently moved into their New York City apartment (which, for most couples, is a very small space). In fact, Ted and his mother had caught Amy in bed with another man in their apartment, which basically was the final straw that led them to seek help. To complete the yarn, Ted added that he was sick of "the perfunctory 0.7 minutes of oral sex prior to the bimonthly intercourse."

Amy wasn't lying when she said that they would work hard, although one might argue that lots of yelling and screaming might not constitute hard work. However, the catharsis seemed to help, and over the next few weeks, they did some great work on forgiveness, trust, and, as much as possible, "wiping the slate clean and starting over."

I taught them about process versus content, and the concept of negative escalation, where one party responds to another's negative statement with a more-potent one, leading the initial party to, essentially, "up the ante." This basically creates a negative cycle where an almost-subconscious contest begins to see who can generate the most negative statements/energy possible. When couples agree to attempt to make note of this phenomenon in their own relationship, the sheer recognition of it can diffuse the buildup:

Wrong

Amy: I've asked you not to wear your hair that way. It makes you look gay and makes me feel like some sort of fag hag.

Ted: Believe me, I'd love to be gay right now. I wouldn't be here with you.

Amy: True. You'd also then be poor and still a drunk.

Ted: Yes, but at least I'd be getting laid by someone who knows how to pleasure a penis!

Right

Amy: I've asked you not to wear your hair that way. It makes you look gay and makes me feel like some sort of fag hag.

Ted: Believe me, I'd love to be gay right now. I wouldn't be here with you.

Amy: [pause]

Ted: [*pause*]

Amy: Is this one of those times that Dr. Rob told us about?

Ted: I think so.

Amy: Me, too. What are we fighting about again?

Ted: Something about me being gay.

Amy: Right. This is probably a stupid argument to be having, given that we have other, more important problems.

Ted: True . . . Do you want to have sex?

Amy: Not really. I'm not sure why, but I kind of want to go shopping with you.

I was really enjoying my work with them. But because Amy and Ted were in such crisis when we started, there wasn't much opportunity to get a lot of background about them and their individual histories. When things started to calm down a bit between the two of them and the sessions weren't all-out screaming banshee-fests, I deemed it a good time to go back and fill in some of the blanks.

"I haven't really gotten a chance to know the two of you outside of the conflict that you've been going through. Now that things are more stable, I'd like to go back to some questions that I might normally ask during the introductory sessions. Specifically, I'd like to know more about how you met, your relationships with your immediate family members, your education, what you do for recreation, things like that."

Amy and Ted filled me in on the relevant details, chronicling what seemed to be a fairly standard middle-class life history. Both had good relationships with their families, were college graduates, met in a bar in their late twenties, had been married about fifteen years, no children, and so on. Eventually, I asked them about work: "Now, if I remember correctly, you work in retail, Ted. Is that right?"

"Yes. My training is in law, but truth be told, I was disbarred a few years ago for alcohol-related problems on the job."

"I'm sorry to hear that. Are you still having these types of problems?"

"No, I've been pretty active in AA, been sober for about eighteen months now," he said.

"Congratulations. And Amy, I know you aren't working now, as we discussed during our first phone consultation, but your profession is in film?"

"Yes, I do some production-type things."

"I'm not quite sure what that means, actually."

Amy looked a little flustered. "I help to produce movies."

"Oh, now I see. You're a sort of production assistant?"

"Sort of."

We seemed to be having an unnecessarily vague exchange. "I'm sorry," I said. "I don't mean to pry unnecessarily, but what do you mean, 'sort of'?"

"Well, I'm a producer, a film producer, um, yes."

"A film producer."

"Yes."

"What sorts of films do you produce?"

"Well, none right now because, as we talked about, I'm between jobs."

My suspicion was growing. "Right, we did talk about that. Have you produced anything I might have seen?"

Amy let out a defeated sigh, realizing that I had won a contest in which I wasn't aware I was a participant. "I suppose you could just Google me to find out, so I'll tell you. Most recently I produced *M——*."

M—— was a top-ten-grossing film for the year it was released, making millions upon millions of dollars. I quickly tried to process this new information, recognizing now that she was a large-scale film executive. Her name wasn't famous to me, but clearly this woman was important in the entertainment industry.

The thought of Dan bitching about his "pittance" of a year-end bonus entered my mind, and one of my many flaws—intolerance for greed—began to emerge. "Amy, how much money did you make on that movie?"

These words came out without recognition, or perhaps simply not a care, of how uncomfortable the topic of money is to some people. My job requires me to ask personal questions all the time, but I almost always preface them with a rationale, as well as a connection to how it might help the therapy. But once I realized that this woman had been pulling the wool over my eyes, I immediately went on the attack.

"What . . . what do you mean?" she said.

"Just that. I'd like to know how much money you made on that film."

"Why is that relevant?" she asked, getting defensive as I became more assertive in my questioning.

"It is relevant because it is important for me to know what sort of lifestyle you two lead. It is also relevant because I agreed to work with you for a fee that I do not offer to people, specifically because I was led to believe that you and your husband are in dire straits, both emotionally and financially. Thus, for this therapy to continue without feelings of suspicion and resentment on my part, I would like to know what your yearly income was last year."

Amy relented quickly, most likely due to the fact that I suggested that our work, which was almost entirely positive, might not be able to continue. "Last year I made about eight million dollars." Mouth agape, staring at her with a combination of shock, disgust, and even envy at her success, I said, "Am I to understand that you haggled me down to nearly $100 less per session than is customary, despite the fact that you made, perhaps in one month, more money than most people will see in their entire lifetime?"

"I told you, I am not working right now."

"You didn't answer my question!" I said, my voice rising in anger.

"Yes, yes—okay. Are you happy?"

"No, I am very *not* happy. I feel taken advantage of and misled. In fact, when are you producing your next film?"

Again, she sighed. "I will be starting work again in two months."

"Is this another high-budget film that will generate a large sum of money for you?"

"Yes, it is."

Finally, I looked at Ted. "Why did you two mislead me?"

Quickly Ted was ready to point the finger. "It wasn't me! She's the cheap one."

"Ted, shut up!" Amy said, the beginning of what could have been negative escalation had the conversation not involved me so directly. "Look, I work very hard for my money, and I like to keep it; is that so wrong?"

"I'm not even sure I'm willing to address that question right now. We need to make a few things clear here if we are going to continue. I think it's fair to say that you were leading me to believe you were poor, or at least, that you were struggling right now with your finances, which is clearly not the case. It is very difficult for us to work together successfully if I can't trust you to tell me the truth on basic issues like general financial status."

"But we've worked well together so far without your knowing the truth, haven't we?"

Sadly, this was true. But when a therapist makes an accommodation, he needs to believe that it is done in good faith by both parties. No one can argue with Steve when he says that we need to pay our expenses through our job, and clients far too often forget that. They sometimes need to be reminded that it's by helping them that we support our own lifestyles. This is independent of whether a private therapist charges $30 per session (unusual, but not unheard of) or $600 (highly unusual, yet still done). So when a mental health professional takes a pay cut for a client, he wants to believe it is fair, ethical, and necessary. If not, resentment can begin to grow, which could ultimately impact the work. For me, "resentment" wasn't even an accurate term for what I felt. Fair or not, "super-ridiculous-off-the-charts-going-to-stab-someone-in-the-face resentment" was a more accurate fit. And although it wasn't necessarily my place to do so, I wanted to teach them a lesson. Dropping them into a vat of acid would have done the trick, but something that benefited others would be a more professional way to conduct myself.

"Yes, Amy, you have a fair point. But—therapy needs to be based on honesty between both parties. The bottom line is that what you led me to believe was not true. I lowered my fee because I believed you truly needed it, and that is simply not the case. You owe me a few hundred dollars. But, while I'm certainly not rich like you, I am not in absolute need of that money. If we are going to continue to work together, starting today, you will pay me my regular fee. The money that you would have owed me, however, will be donated to a worthy charity. I think that would be a nice thing to do for the community, and quite frankly, I think it will show you how wrong it is to do what you did."

Amy looked at the floor like a teenager who had come home four hours after curfew and was about to be grounded. And the reality was that I was treating her like one, holding a moral cross over her. "Fine," she said.

Ted seemed like he couldn't care less that they needed to make amends, and that it was a perfectly reasonable request. "Sure," he said.

"Where do you think that money should go?"

Amy looked up. "The 92nd Street Y is always looking for donations."

The 92nd Street Y is one of the most prosperous organizations in New York City. Celebrities send their children there to learn about world history, Western culture, and various forms of high art. There were other organizations with a much greater need.

"With all due respect," I said, "the Y doesn't need anything from you or me. They are just fine. How about something that might improve the lives of those less fortunate, rather than making people with an embarrassment of riches slightly more comfortable?"

I knew I was being judgmental toward the wealthy, the financial cream of the crop, but again, remembering Dan's greed at his year-end bonus years before and now seeing Ted and Amy's egregious actions made me simply not care.

"Like what?" Ted asked.

"How about a poor school in an impoverished area?" I said.

"Do you donate to them?" Amy asked, with a hint of sarcasm in her voice.

"I do now, because it's my money we're using to donate, isn't it?"

By that point Amy had had enough. She left in a huff with Ted in tow, saying that she needed to "think about it." But, two weeks later they returned with a thank-you note in hand from a local school. Apparently the money was going to be used to buy new textbooks for grade-school children in a very indigent area. I was both a bit surprised and very proud of them. They could have just refused to face the music and found someone new to work with, but here they were, holding what amounted to a written atonement. They also deserved praise for dealing with their sanctimonious therapist.

"I want to apologize to both of you if I suggested that you are bad people for what you did."

"You did, in fact, do that," Amy said, "but we deserved it."

"I don't believe either of you are bad, but your actions were unacceptable. In other words, I don't mean to label *you*, but rather what you *did*. Can we get past this and continue our work together?"

Both Ted and Amy were eager to continue, and so we recommenced therapy. And through improving their communication, the marriage improved. The affairs stopped as well, supporting the cliché that often extramarital intercourse is not the actual problem, but rather a symptom of difficulty within the marriage. When Ted's mother moved out, stating that the house was "getting boring without all the fighting and extramarital sex," we all decided that Amy and Ted were ready to cease therapy and go about their better, healthier, and extremely prosperous lives.

6 p.m.
A Victim for Life?

During my third year of graduate school, a good friend who was one of my classmates was in a nasty car accident. She was run off a two-lane highway by an eighteen-wheeler in the rural outskirts of Toledo. As her vehicle left the macadam and she drove onto the ancillary dirt, her car flipped over multiple times, leaving her upside down in the driver's seat with no one nearby to assist her.

Save for various cuts, scrapes, and bruises, she wasn't hurt. But looking out of a shattered glass window, blood flowing up into her head as her seat belt kept her in the upside-down position, she was terrified. She later told me that after the first flip of the vehicle she immediately believed completely and fully that her life was over. And when she found herself still breathing, she had no idea what to think.

Cell phones were fairly new then, but fortunately she had one. She dialed 911 and waited. She was pulled from the car by the ambulance crew and taken to the hospital for treatment. She called me from there after some bandaging and I drove out to pick her up the next morning.

She asked me to take her to the impound lot where her car was located. When we got to it we quickly realized that it was essentially scrap metal; you never would have guessed that anyone who had been inside of it would be alive, let alone without a single broken bone. Upon seeing the car, my friend burst into tears.

We went out for drinks that night and she said that she didn't want to talk about it. "It's done, over," she said.

Two nights later, however, she started to have nightmares about the accident. Dreams are rarely facsimiles of our exact lives, but each night involved her either dying, being maimed, or having something taken away from her, such as a purse or toy from when she was a young girl. We used *very* rudimentary dream-analysis skills to interpret the items that were taken away as a loss of innocence and perhaps naiveté. In other words, the accident had quickly changed her from a safe, secure, and somewhat unaware woman into a new person who suddenly recognized that life can be taken away, or at least significantly altered, through a simple turn of events.

After my friend became hesitant and ultimately fearful of driving, she and I sat down to talk about her state of mind and lack of well-being. Psychology graduate students are in a strange position at this point in their training. Like most people, we know that something is wrong, and we also have a clue as to what to do about it. However, we're not qualified to actually provide any real treatment, and are often left wondering what the best course of action would be.

"I think you need to talk about the accident; you need to process it," I said.

"I know, I know," she said, milking a beer in the local pub. "I'm just an anxious mess. I think about the accident all the time. If something had happened to me, my family would never have recovered."

Although neither of us introduced the term, we were both concerned about her developing post-traumatic stress disorder (PTSD). Most people commonly associate this condition with rapes and assaults, as well as war experiences. But it's really a condition that involves any trauma, defined by the DSM-IV as "an event or events that involved actual or threatened death or serious injury, or a threat to the physical integrity of self or others," and said trauma is really in the eyes of the one who experiences it. I've seen clients get into horrific car accidents and see brutal violence yet not demonstrate any symptoms of PTSD (although one could argue that these people were still seriously impacted). Others, however, have developed symptoms based on more "benign" incidents, where there was only a potential for harm with no significant outcome. Every person responds to events differently.

PTSD is generally highlighted by three major symptom clusters:

1. *Reexperience: My friend began to have nightmares, but reexperiencing can occur in the form of intrusive thoughts, feelings of reoccurrence, or even a physiological reaction when presented with cues that symbolize the event (e.g., experiencing extreme anxiety when sitting in the driver's seat of a car).*

2. *Avoidance: After the accident she wanted to avoid all conversation about what had happened. She also wanted to "block out" many parts of the event so that she didn't need to think about them. Because avoidance can serve as a temporary form of relief, it unfortunately reinforces a lack of processing. In some cases, avoidance can become generalized; for example, my friend ultimately could have avoided driving on all roads similarly constructed, or even driving altogether.*

3. *Increased arousal: Many people with PTSD show signs of being easily irritated and hypervigilant, and exhibit an exaggerated startle response. For a few weeks following the accident, my friend would become jumpy and anxious when she heard the revving of a car engine or the squealing of brakes.*

Why do these symptoms occur? Remember Sara and her grief. The brain is designed to "make sense" of everything that happens to it. It likes to work, to process, to put things into perspective. If you consciously attempt to avoid doing this, your brain will fight you on it. Intrusive thoughts and nightmares occur because the brain is essentially saying *You need to think about this!* There is a natural tendency for avoidance because the opposite is usually quite painful; who would *choose* to relive something traumatic that is already over? But when the information isn't completely digested by the brain, it is duped into thinking that the trauma might not really be over. Hence the hypervigilance and exaggerated startle response. The sound of the engine got my friend thinking *Am I back there, in the car? Is another accident about to happen?*

I pushed my friend to talk about the accident, in detail, to help her to process what had happened to her. I encouraged her to work against the notion of "It's in the past; put it behind you and try to forget," which is the advice that many people receive when they've had a horrendous experience. But if you look at research studies from people returning from Afghanistan or Iraq, or from those who have been beaten or raped, it's immediately apparent that without talking through the thoughts and emotions, symptoms tend to emerge. And while some challenge this "debriefing" philosophy, citing that it can in fact induce symptoms of PTSD rather than mitigate them, in my personal and professional life I have yet to see this occur.

My friend ultimately decided to simply tell the story of the accident, over and over, to anyone who would listen. She would go about it in great detail: what she did that morning, what she ate, her clothes, the music she listened to in the car before the accident, the moment she noticed the truck, her thoughts about death as she swerved off the road, the good-byes she said to her family as the car flipped over and over, and ultimately the confusion she felt when she realized that she was unhurt. By continuing to process this information aloud, her preliminary symptoms of anxiety and her nightmares abated. My friend survived the psychological aftermath.

Soon after I started my own practice, I began treating a woman whom I'll call Deb, a twenty-year-old sophomore at a local university. She had been a victim of date rape a few months prior. Deb had met a fellow student at a party and agreed to go out with him the following weekend. After a night of wining and dining they ended up back at his room. While she agreed to be physical with him, she stated that she asked him not to let things go too far. Against her wishes, he ultimately penetrated her.

After the event she had done what so many people who have been traumatized attempt to do: forget. This precipitated many symptoms, including isolating herself, crying spells, nightmares, a fear of dating, avoidance of people who even looked like the perpetrator, and even self-hate. *I'm damaged goods now. This is my fault; I never should have looked good. I shouldn't have had any wine, or gone to his room. I deserve this. I'm a slut.* This went on almost incessantly for weeks.

After you've been in the field for a time it is easy to erroneously assume that everyone thinks like a shrink. *PTSD, of course. Her symptoms are a result of the trauma and her inability to process what happened to her. She must know this as well as I do; it's just common sense.* And with a seemingly infinite amount of information available through various media, it's easy to believe that everyone is up to speed on common psychological problems. So when she held back tears and asked, "What the fuck is wrong with me? Why am I like this?" I was taken aback. *She needs me to explain all of this to her. She needs to hear what is wrong and that it can be treated.*

It was then that I realized how quickly therapy begins. It's not when you sit down and say, "Okay, here's what we're going to do." It starts as soon as you speak with each other and she begins to tell you why she needs help. She's not only traumatized but confused and fearful about what's going to happen to her. She needs not only information but hope.

"This is what we call PTSD," I said.

She looked confused. "Like shell shock?"

"Exactly, just like in war," I said.

She paused. "If there's a name for this," she said, "that means other people have it. I'm not alone."

This is the psychological concept known as universality, seen in my work with the grieving widow, Sara. Provided that the clinician doesn't invalidate someone's personal experience by lumping her in with everyone else who has come through the door, it can be a powerful therapeutic tool.

"Of course you're not alone. And I think therapy would be very helpful for you."

"What do I have to do?" she asked.

"Actually, I'm going to give you some material to read on PTSD, written by some of the graduate students here, but for the most part you are going to be doing a lot of talking."

"About what happened to me?"

"Yes. I'll need you to talk a lot about what happened to you."

"I don't like the sound of that. That's what I've been trying to avoid."

"Many people do exactly that. But this is what is contributing so much to your struggles right now: the poor sleep, the nightmares, the crying spells. We can do something about it." I handed her a three-page document. "This material talks a little bit about PTSD and what we're going to do in therapy. Would you read it before our next session, so we can talk about it? And please know that under no circumstances will we do anything that you are not aware of beforehand or don't feel you can handle."

This treatment can never be thrust down someone's throat. Most clients are very hesitant to begin PTSD work because they have to do the very thing they've gotten good at dodging, which is processing the event. In some ways it is similar to an elevator phobia. The person knows he has to get into the elevator to feel better, and yet ironically that's the last thing he can do.

Deb agreed to read the information and think it over. It explained to her the underpinnings of avoidance, reexperiencing, and increased arousal. It also talked about the type of therapy we would be doing, called prolonged exposure therapy (PET). Essentially, this type of treatment asks people to "relive" the experience in the therapy room, in a safe environment. Deb would describe the event in great detail over extended periods of time. We would record our sessions, and Deb would be asked to listen to the tapes between sessions. The approach has several benefits:

1. *It helps to organize the events and "make sense" of them, especially when new information is revealed as details are remembered.*
2. *Negative feelings that get triggered decrease (known as "habituation"). As the client describes the events, the reactions that decrease quality of life, such as anger and anxiety, begin to subside.*
3. *When the client learns how to manage the feelings, she is able to remember the event without a perceived loss of control. While it's impossible to "forget" what happened, clients who engage in this therapy often feel a sense of being able to file away the event when they don't want to think about it. Again, this is similar to grief, as clients who have completed the process often report the ability to put aside the thoughts and emotions for extended periods of time.*

The last question Deb had for me before she left her first session was, "I have a feeling that this will get worse before it gets better; is that right?"

"It's possible. When we try to suppress things and then relinquish them we bring up a lot of new feelings. It could be hard at first. It's like if you broke a bone and it didn't heal properly. We need to reset it, and that could be painful. But I promise that I'll be there to help you through it, step by step."

Deb sighed. "I have trouble imagining feeling worse than this. Life has been very hard since this happened. I'll try. That's all I can say."

Deb left at that point but was already in a better position. She had information, a plan of action, and a professional—albeit a somewhat inexperienced one—in her corner to help her follow through. She was teed up for success.

When clients with PTSD begin PET, the anxiety associated with telling their story can be overwhelming for them. Much like David and his OCD symptoms, clients will often do anything possible to eliminate the negative feelings associated with the trauma, meaning they will usually tear through the narrative as quickly as possible, never giving themselves a chance to process what happened to them:

We went on a date. He took me out to dinner. I had some drinks and we flirted. Then we went back to his place. At first it was okay, but then he started to go too far. I told him to stop but he wouldn't. He kept going and forced me to have sex with him.

When clients are struggling like this, it's important to give them an important message: Tell me a story—a full, complete story, with a beginning, middle, and end. Pretend that you are a writer and give me every single detail that you can think of. Take me there; pretend I'm standing with you the entire time. This directive can sometimes help clients to slow down and take their time, although the anxiety remains a driving force, urging them to complete the tale (i.e., the quicker the story is told, the sooner the nervous feelings will dissipate). To combat this, clients are told in advance that the *entire* session will be dedicated to the story. In other words, if the story only takes one minute, then the client should plan on telling the story forty-five times.

Deb, however, was unlike any client I had ever seen, before or since. After the first session she clearly had done some significant soul-searching, realizing that this work was important. As a creative writing student she could easily give great details about very mundane experiences, let alone such a significant trauma. As we sat down and I pressed PLAY on the recorder, Deb took a deep breath and began to tell me what happened:

"I met Gary at a party the week before, at a frat. He was one of those guys who looked confident, but you could see that layer of insecurity. He rolled his sleeves up just a bit too far to show off his biceps, popped his collar, wore his hair over his eyes in a way that said 'I don't care what my hair looks like,' but you just knew that he had some feelings about himself that weren't all that great.

"I don't know why I agreed to go out with him; insecurity isn't my thing. He was cute, though, and popular, in one of the best fraternities. Why not, you know? What could go wrong?"

Deb paused at that point and looked past me, to a vacant spot on the wall.

"Deb, you okay?" I asked.

She squeezed her eyes shut. "Uh-huh," she said and breathed in and out a few times. It is crucial to continue at these moments, because clients are used to freezing the story, pressing PAUSE to suppress the pain, and going about their day as best they can. Deb had somehow decided that her story wasn't stopping. She continued as the faint sound of the tape recorder hummed at my side.

"I wore tight jeans and a halter top. I figured I should dress in a way that made him want me. I already knew that we'd probably fool around a bit, and that I should give him a taste of what he could have if he played his cards right. I like dating, I like sex; I thought it would be fun with him. I'm not a prude, but I make men wait a few dates. They don't respect you otherwise.

"So I looked good. As soon as he came to my dorm and his eyes lit up when he saw me, I knew I looked good. 'You look amazing,' he said, clearly impressed.

"We went out to dinner, some cheap Italian place down on Fifth. I remember the sign was buzzing and the 'L' in the name was out, but I can't remember what it was called. All throughout dinner he was eyeing me, looking me up and down, and focusing on my chest a lot. I didn't mind. It was flattering. The place didn't even card us, so booze wasn't a problem. I had . . . three, no four glasses of some cheap red wine. He had three and then stopped because he was driving, but I'm sure he had a buzz going.

"We flirted throughout the whole night. I knew where it was going, at least in terms of what he wanted. *I'll give him something to bring him back for more. Hooking up with a popular frat guy wouldn't be so bad for a few months.*

"When we left the restaurant he had his arm around me. 'I've got some new CDs,' he said. 'Let's go back to my place and I can show you my room and we'll listen to music.' I smiled and said, 'Okay, as long as you keep your hands to yourself.' I knew that he wouldn't, but I wanted to give him a signal that he wasn't getting laid that night—that he'd have to put in some effort if he wanted the complete package.'"

Again Deb paused and looked at the ground. "Rob, why are girls like me so stupid?"

Deb began to tap into the myriad cognitive errors that victims create in their minds. Here she's beginning to look into her role in what happened. And while it's hard to argue that she put herself in an extremely dangerous position, it was just a matter of time before she gave herself 100 percent of the blame and took on complete responsibility for someone else's actions.

Before I had a chance to speak, she went on. "We went to his apartment. He didn't live in the frat house and he had roommates, but no one was home. It was actually in a really bad area of town, near the projects. It was definitely somewhere I wouldn't hang around by myself. 'Ah, it's just before midnight,' he said. 'Let's have a beer before the day ends.'

"We stood in the kitchen and drank the beer. After a few sips, he leaned in. 'You look fucking great.' He smelled like pasta, beer, wine, and the Gap all at the same time. It wasn't bad; he had a bit of a slur in his voice, but I was at least somewhat turned on. Fuck, I'm so stupid. So fucking stupid." And suddenly she burst into tears. With no attempt to cover her eyes or reach for a tissue, pure anguish came out. "THAT FUCKING ASSHOLE, THAT STUPID FUCKING ASSHOLE!" she shouted, a loud scream that echoed throughout the office.

One of my professors stressed the importance of not interrupting the flow of the client's narrative. Even though Deb had deviated from the plot of the story, she was definitely processing more fully than she had before. And if she had given me any sense that she felt unsafe or was speaking out of bounds, I would have corrected her and encouraged her to speak as freely as possible.

Eventually Deb reached for a tissue, wiped her eyes, and blew her nose. Another few deep breaths and she continued.

"He kissed me, or we kissed together. Whatever—it doesn't matter. It was really deep kissing, a little too aggressive. And within two seconds I felt his hand slide into the front of my jeans. No buildup, no foreplay, nothing. He just grabbed my fucking crotch. I immediately pulled back and tried to laugh it off a bit, something like 'Hey, easy there, guy. I don't think we're going there just yet.'

"And he said, 'I think we are.'

"It was right then, Rob, that I got a little scared," she said. But I could see anger in her eyes as she said it. Probably the same feeling that had emerged when she began yelling. This time she wanted to control it a bit. That was okay, because I knew the feeling would return in due time.

"I thought that I could try to just run past him, out of the kitchen and into the street. But even if that worked, I'd be in the middle of Shit Town and probably would have gotten stabbed. I think he knew this and said, 'You can go if you want.' He even stepped aside and swept his arm across the room to show me it was okay to pass. 'But you don't want to be out there alone. You're safer with me. If you just give me what I want I can take you home.'

"I thought about taking out my cell phone and calling a cab, but then he came forward again. I didn't know what to do. I was drunk, originally turned-on, now scared and confused. Would he actually hurt me? Why I did this, I have no fucking idea, but I offered a deal. 'I'll give you a hand job, but that's it,' I said to him.

"It was almost as if he were anticipating an offer because he immediately said, 'I want to finger you while you do it.' And I just nodded so that we could get things going, and over with, as soon as possible. We walked into the bedroom and I took off my pants. It was so businesslike. He came in and lay on his back on the bed. He undid his jeans and took out his penis. And then he . . ."

Deb paused again and her voice got shaky. "He licked his palm and fingers and stuck two fingers up in me. He pulled me down on the bed and put my hand on his penis, so I started stroking it. He was pushing unusually fast with his fingers so I started doing the same thing for him with my hand. Rob," she said. "I suddenly felt a contraction, almost like I came."

She hung her head in shame, elbows on her knees. Victims of sexual abuse often need to be educated that the body can respond and feel pleasure despite the lack of psychological arousal or even with feelings of disgust or revulsion. I didn't immediately interject because it was more important to let the narrative run its course.

"Fuck. When that happened he got so turned on. He must have thought he had won me over or something. Or maybe it just pushed him over the edge. He immediately rolled on top of me and said, 'I have to. I have to fuck you now.'

"It's not like he was some gigantic football player or something, but when he held my arms down and let his weight fall on me, he felt like a ton of bricks. I didn't scream but I remember saying, 'No.' Just once. It could have been a thousand times and it wouldn't have made a fucking difference. I didn't even feel scared at that point. I was resigned to it. I got myself into this spot and I was paying the price. So stupid. He slipped into me, pumped away maybe ten times, pulled out, and came on my shirt. My first thought was 'You can't even last, you loser,' but I was glad it was over. He fell on me, kissed my neck, and then rolled over. After he caught his breath he got up and went into the bathroom.

"I didn't move. I just stayed there with my pants off and the cum on my shirt.

"I heard the toilet flush and he came out. 'I'll take you home now,' he said. I sat up and pulled on my pants. I took one look at him, knowing that I was just a statistic at this point. My life would never be the same.

"I left. Just walked past him into the living room and out the door, into the streets. I didn't care what happened to me at that point. I just walked and walked. At one point some guy in the street yelled something about how good I looked. I just kept going, walking mindlessly, and after a half-hour or so, I was home."

Deb and I sat silently for a few moments, each of us processing what had just happened. Then the recorder clicked. Out of tape.

"I've never told anyone the entire story before," she said.

"I really don't want this to sound like a stupid question," I said, "but can you tell me how you're feeling right now, having shared that?"

"A little edgy," she said. "During the story there were times I felt calm and safe, but other times I got extremely anxious and angry."

"Were those anxious and angry feelings similar to those you experienced during the trauma?"

"Oh yes, absolutely."

"That's the reexperiencing piece we talked about. I know you don't want to hear this, but if we go through this over and over, the body and brain will start to recognize that the trauma is actually over and will stop responding this way."

She looked at me with some trepidation. "How many times do we need to do this?"

Pinning down a number of sessions is always difficult, and I always hate admitting that fact to clients. It creates a feeling of inadequacy in me, even though I know that each person's needs are both different and unpredictable.

"The truth is that I'm not sure," I said. "For some people it's as small as just a few sessions. Others go through it dozens of times. That being said, you were able to give very specific details about your trauma. That's good. Many people have blocked out parts of it, and it takes many repetitions to get those details out. If you listen to the tape from today a few times each week, I think you'll feel better sooner."

It's understandable when clients are unable to follow through with this type of therapy. The memories, the suffering, the addictive quality of the brief relief that comes from avoiding—all of these things make it hard to stay the course. Some people do, in fact, get worse in the beginning as we begin to "stir the pot" of emotions that are suppressed.

Deb wouldn't allow that to happen to her. Every day she listened to the tape, and every week she told her story. Now and then a detail would be corrected ("No, he looked at me with disdain at that moment, not seduction") or a new fact would emerge ("I looked down at my untied shoelace as I walked home, not caring"). And after two months, Deb was significantly less symptomatic.

Like many others with PTSD, Deb experienced what are often referred to as "stuck points." These are maladaptive and faulty thoughts about the trauma and its ramifications. As predicted, Deb would report, "I get these flashes of words in my head. They say, 'It's all your fault.' And that's true. If I wasn't dressed like a whore, and buzzed, and I didn't go into his apartment, this wouldn't have happened."

The therapist's job here is unbridled challenging. "No. You made choices that were not sound," I said, leaning forward. "Those choices put you in a bad position. But that didn't give him the right, the duty, or the obligation to make you suffer for those choices. For whatever reason, he made the decision to hurt you. You and I are going to restructure that erroneous thought. Let's change 'It's all my fault' to a more accurate statement."

Deb thought. She was at a point where the tears were gone and her focus was intact. She was angry at him and had a right to that. She just needed to say it aloud, with conviction. "I did some dumb things, but that doesn't mean I deserved to be raped. He is solely responsible for the outcome that occurred."

"Say more," I said.

"I don't know if he's sick, a psychopath, or just an asshole, but he didn't have any right. No fucking right."

"How does that feel?" I asked.

"A little better, a little more . . . powerful."

I strongly encouraged Deb to repeat those words to herself on a daily basis. And when she did, she got closer to where she needed to be.

Much like the way I had struggled with mental imagery of Janet with other men, Deb would sometimes focus too much on the worst parts of the trauma. Of course, these are where the most painful details are, but she needed to have a narrative with equal attention paid to all parts. At first her story would sometimes become vague when she recounted being away from the perpetrator, in a safer place, after the trauma was over. This was unacceptable. Like Carol had taught me, she needed to "finish the movie." I pushed her as much as possible to focus on the moments when she had told her friends and family, and how supportive they were. She tattooed images in her head of being safe in session with me. She needed to remember, clearly and fully, that there was a Deb before the trauma occurred and that there would still be a Deb afterward. Those pictures needed to be clear in her head.

When the story had a complete beginning, middle, and end, and when all the pieces were in place, Deb had processed what had happened in the most comprehensive way possible. She corrected her errors in thinking and assigned the blame where it needed to be with greater ease than when she first began treatment. She stopped viewing herself as "damaged goods," and realized that even though she'd had this horrific sexual experience, she was not made of glass and would ultimately be okay. She began dating again and allowed herself to get comfortable with men who were trustworthy. When she got to that point, it was time to say good-bye.

The goal of the treatment is not to forget what happened; far from it. Memories shape who we are, so the mission statement is not to create an *Eternal Sunshine of the Spotless Mind* scenario. Rather, our objective was to give Deb greater control over her memories. It's not as if after therapy was over she never thought about her trauma. Of course she did, especially when she saw the perpetrator or even one of his fraternity brothers. But before she started therapy, the cognitions, images, and emotions had flooded her being; she didn't know what to do with them. After therapy, the experience became much more manageable. When reminded of the trauma, she thought about what happened, but like Sara, she now had the power to move the memory into the filing cabinet and slide the drawer shut. That's what therapy gave her, and her quality of life is significantly better because of it.

7 p.m.
Sexual Deviants, Angry Spouses, and a Neophyte Shrink Without a Clue

In my second year of graduate school, my classmates and I geared up for what was known as "placement time." Up until this point in our training, we had only done basic psychological testing and some short-term therapy with students in our university clinic. Placement time was the day that you received your assignment for your third-year practicum—the year that you went out into the community to get more hands-on, direct clinical experience. Generally, these jobs were about twenty hours per week, and the student worked with more-severe psychological difficulties. "Front-line stuff," one of my professors called it. If you were lucky, you could go across town to the prestigious medical school with the third-year psychiatry residents and wear impressive nametags with the hospital logo on it. If you were me, you went somewhere else.

In my case, that meant heading Up North. Up North involved traveling over the border into Michigan, a one-hour commute each way, while all of my classmates were making five-minute drives around Toledo. Up North meant working at a small community mental health center in the middle of nowhere for about $900 per month. It also involved doing the job that every student feared and/or loathed: treating sex offenders.

"Get ready to control your urge to punch a forty-five-year-old man in the face when he tells you how much he enjoyed orally molesting a nine-month-old," I was told by Kate, the third-year student who was just starting to wrap up her yearlong purgatory Up North. "You're really going to hate it. Damn, I pity you."

"Why did the faculty pick me?" I asked her.

"The same reason they picked me. You're a pushover; they knew you wouldn't say no," she said. And she was right. If I had refused and dug my heels in, there was always a possibility that I could go unassigned for the year. This would mean less experience, which would be noted when it came time to apply for internships and postdoctoral fellowships. When the faculty needed someone who wouldn't call their bluff, they knew where to turn.

That September, I trekked Up North, and within the first few hours of my first day, my life became all about sexual deviancy. (Note: Sexual offending and deviancy varies by culture, but it generally assumes a lack of consent by the offender's partner. It is also assumed that children are incapable of giving consent. While specific statistics vary, it should be noted that sexual offending is almost exclusively a male disorder.)

My supervisor for the year was a middle-aged, attractive, and immensely confident woman. She immediately knew that I was beyond unskilled in this area of psychology. My young, red face, full of anxiety and the effects of Vaseline from years prior, told her I was in completely over my head, full of embarrassment and confusion. And because I was accustomed to very supportive, nurturing faculty like Dr. Charles, who had helped me develop my skills for empathy, her stern and unempathic take on my naiveté made me feel like I was working with Nurse Ratched.

"So, Mr. Dobrenski, tell me what you know about sex?" she said within minutes of our first meeting.

"I . . . I don't know what you mean."

"You don't know what I mean?" She cupped her hands over her mouth to make a de facto megaphone. "S . . . E . . . X?" she said loudly.

"You mean like how babies are made?"

"No. Talk to me about sex toys, fantasies, punching while fucking, anal, those sorts of things."

I blanched. Actually I probably turned redder than my standard ruddy look. In reality I'm sure I did both, making my face the color of a nice rosé wine.

"Why are you doing this?" I asked.

"Mr. Dobrenski, we're talking about real life here, not bullshit textbook stuff. If you can't look your partner in the eye at McDonald's and say, 'I love it when you suck me off before I can even get the gag ball in my mouth,' you'll never be completely comfortable doing this type of work."

"But I don't know if I *want* to do this kind of work."

"So do you?"

"Do I what?"

"Like being sucked off pre–gag ball?"

It crossed my mind that what she was saying might qualify as some sort of harassment, but I wasn't mentally strong enough to stand up to her.

"Whatever they're paying you here, I'll double it," I said. "Just please don't torture me like this."

"I want you to understand something," she said. "I make jokes because it's a way for us to cope."

I couldn't recall where in the conversation she had made a joke.

"All therapists do it. It's a way for us to deal with helping, or in some cases, not helping others who are constantly in need. It's a defense mechanism. If we didn't do it, we'd go crazy.

"Look," she continued, "everyone has problems with sex at some point in their lives. During your career you'll hear married people say that they aren't getting enough, or it's too much, or there's not enough variety. You'll listen to single people say they want more intimacy with sex, or to have less one-night stands, or maybe *more* one-night stands. Some people want to use toys, others porn, blah blah blah. You'll eventually hear it all."

She had a confidence talking about sex that I had not seen in anyone before.

"But this, Rob, *this,*" she said, her arm sweeping around the room to indicate the mental health center's scope, "is where real, hard-core sex problems are seen. We are all affected by this."

"I don't understand how we're all affected by . . . this."

"This town, this city, this county, this state, country, and world are all a community. What the men in our clinic have done impact themselves, their victims, their spouses and children. The victims' families are devastated, and when those victims go into relationships, they bring their experiences to the table. So their new partners are affected. Coworkers find out and worry about their own kids, and prevention specialists go into schools and talk to the children and teachers to prevent what could happen to them. *They* are affected. We work with the offenders and therefore don't look at sex the same way anymore, so *we* are affected. The ripple goes outward and outward and outward."

It started to make some sense.

"You are going to start working with men who have done horrible things and have hurt many people. Society thinks of them as monsters, as do many mental health professionals. I don't. I, and hopefully you, will see them as having a psychological disorder. That will allow you to treat them fairly and comprehensively.

"However, make no mistake: Your client is the community. The community's protection comes first. This is the first rule of treating sexual offenders in an outpatient setting, and any clinician who forgets that is grossly negligent. If you suspect an offender is reverting to old behaviors, you are legally and ethically obligated to protect society. In other words, treating sex offenders is a great responsibility, because you are helping everyone. Don't ever forget that."

"I understand."

"I'd also like you to work in a group setting with the spouses or significant others of the offenders."

"These men have spouses?"

"Absolutely. That's the *point*, Mr. Dobrenski. Many sexual offenders aren't the ridiculously creepy man in the van across the street from the school. They are fathers, coaches, and husbands. And you will be helping the women in their lives."

At that moment I couldn't fathom how I could be of help to anyone or anything.

"I have to be very honest with you about the significant others. Very few women are pleased, especially at the onset, to be 'going to fucking group' every week for a disorder that they do not have. Many of the women—and much of society in general—do not even see the offenders as 'ill,' at least not in the way one might view someone with schizophrenia. They are incorrect, but that is their belief. A male group leader—in this case, you—will likely receive very strong transference reactions from the women, who will see you as an easy target for the gamut of negative feelings toward men that they understandably are experiencing. In other words, prepare yourself to be a punching bag for a lot of rage, especially since your fellow student Kate was a woman, so the dynamic for these women will be quite new."

"I really don't think I'm qualified . . ."

Dismissing me with a brief wave of her hand, she continued. "You have to strike a balance between empathizing with their feelings of anger, betrayal, and embarrassment with a confident knowledge of the nature of sexual offending and its underpinnings as an illness that impacts not only the offender and victim but also the community at large. Can you do that?"

"Actually I'm pretty sure I can*not* do that. I'm not even sure what you're talking about."

"How old are you, Mr. Dobrenski?"

"I'll be twenty-six very soon."

"How soon?"

"Ten months."

"And your experience with sexual deviance work extends . . . ?"

"About as long as this conversation."

"All right then. You look like you're about eight and have virtually nothing to offer in terms of life experience or knowledge to these women, who are victims in their own right. As your supervisor I will guide you along as best as I can, but I don't have the time to watch you from moment to moment like they do at the university clinic. You're going to need to do a lot of this on your own."

I'm sure I looked panic-stricken and in need of deep breathing exercises or an illicit substance to calm down, so she took my hand and her firm, coldly clinical, and almost cyborg-sounding voice softened a little. "Rob, you'll do this, and you'll thank me someday for my tough love. Remember, no matter how many books on support groups or frotteurism you read, you need the growing pains of practicing as a professional."

"What's frotteurism?"

"It usually involves sexually touching and rubbing against nonconsensual partners."

"Who does something like that?" I asked, resisting the urge to pull away in disgust at her calmness with this situation.

She took her hand away. "Some of your new clients do something like that, so get comfortable with it. I will tell you this again and again until it sticks: Don't hide from what's different and scary."

I left that meeting confused and nervous, with a lot of questions and hardly any answers. I hadn't chosen to run these groups and didn't yet see what an amazing challenge and growth opportunity it would be. All I envisioned at the time were perverted men who were coaches during the day and predators at night. But that wasn't quite right. My supervisor said they had "disorders." But what, exactly, were their diseases? Did they simply have behavioral problems, or was it biochemical? Did they have structural abnormalities in their brains? Was this a simple issue of power, like all the anti-rape posters suggested? Apparently, due to budget limitations, all the offenders were given the same treatment, whether they were a frotteur or a pedophile. Could that possibly work?

The initial conclusion I drew was to share my supervisor's opinion that the men were "ill," even if I didn't know exactly what that meant. And although not every illness presents itself in a way that pulls at your heartstrings, if I could remember that I was dealing with mental pathology, I could possibly be of service.

And what about the spouses? I didn't know what to think about them. "Victims in their own right"? If so, why did they choose to stay in their relationships? I was sure many of them had children and didn't want to break up their families. Others were probably scared to be alone. Some probably truly loved their husbands and wanted to help them. In all likelihood, most of the women were probably a combination of all of these types, and didn't know what the hell to do about this issue. This I could understand, and I suddenly felt sorry for them for being in such a horrible place. If I could just remember that feeling I'd be in a better position to help them.

Unfortunately, the feeling didn't last, and pure anxiety returned. I had the responsibility of helping a group of people with a problem I knew nothing about and who in all likelihood didn't even want to be there. On my own. With my eight-year-old face. Maybe I would get lucky and they would simply pity me for being a neophyte. Doubtful. On the night before the first group my final thought before falling asleep was "Set the bar low. If they don't castrate you during the first session, consider it a success."

The eight men in our Tuesday group had a range of sexual issues from voyeurism to pedophilia. Two of the patients were convicted rapists. Some of the group members had served prison sentences for their offenses; others had agreed to attend the sessions in lieu of entering jail; and two had just started the adjudication process and had volunteered to join the group on the advice of lawyers who were hoping to curry favor with the court. One of the men had forced fellatio on a two-year-old boy; another climbed trees to stare into people's bedrooms; and yet another had exposed himself to his teenage daughter's friends.

Because of the size of the group and the fact that I was an unlicensed and extremely green graduate student, a second professional ran the group with me. My cotherapist was an already-licensed social worker, a highly skilled and well-seasoned clinician who didn't seem to mind being the only woman in the room.

Our treatment was conducted in an "open group" format, which meant there was no formal beginning or end. Patients could enter the group at any time and would leave once they were deemed "rehabilitated," or they were expelled if they offended again. Thus, on any given night, you might have someone who had been in the group for only a week (a junior) relating his experiences to a patient who had been in the program for more than four years (a senior). Most of the seniors tended to assume leadership roles, confronting other members, acting as a support system, and serving as a beacon of hope that the lifestyle of an offender was not etched in stone.

My introduction to the group by my coleader was less than positive: "This is Rob Dobrenski, a graduate student from UT. He's co-running the group with me for the next nine months. Rob, why don't you tell the group something about yourself and your experience?"

I've never been a good public speaker, and I'd never run a group before. I had no experiences with sex offenders to relate. I didn't even know anyone who had smacked his girlfriend. And here I was, about to introduce myself as a "man" who would help these people overcome a sickness that I knew nothing about. In fact, the way she phrased her introductory question, I had to wonder if she considered me a new patient who should say why I'm sick too.

"Hello . . . there. I'm a twenty-five-year-old . . . Caucasian male. I'm also a third-year graduate student, and I've always been fascinated with sex offenders. Well, not the offenders themselves, but the offenses. I mean, not the offenses per se, but working with people like you . . ."

A senior jumped in. "And what type of people are we, exactly?"

"Um . . . people who I think have made some poor choices in their lives, people who . . . can be . . . rehabilitated?"

"Oh yeah? And what the fuck makes you think that?"

"Well, I assume that's why we're here . . ."

"And your assumption is based on what, Mr. Graduate Student?"

Pause. "Life experience?"

Everyone was left unimpressed.

My work with the women was somewhat different, mainly because I had no cotherapist. As this was considered a "support group," I was allowed by law to conduct it alone. "Support groups" generally differ from "therapy groups" in that they often don't have a specific outline for each session, the members of the group tend to have varying levels of participation and attendance, and their purpose is exactly what it sounds like: to simply provide support to the members who are dealing with a particular issue. Sometimes they are facilitated by nonprofessionals.

The Significant Others of Sexual Offenders Support Group was unique in the sense that enrollment in the group was required. If the significant other wanted her partner to be treated for his sexual offending, she needed to be a part of the group. If she was not there during the regular meeting times, the man was kicked out of treatment, plain and simple. This requirement was based on certain theoretical and guiding principles of the mental health center:

1. *Sexual offenders suffer from a psychological disorder that can, in some cases, be treated via a comprehensive program.*

2. *The process of becoming an offender involves experiencing various psychological problems such as low self-esteem, depression, anxiety, and substance abuse. The process includes certain behavioral problems in addition to the offending, especially lying to both oneself and others.*

3. *Without complete disclosure of the offender's thoughts, feelings, actions, and history of his psychological growth, both sexually and nonsexually, rehabilitation is not possible. This disclosure needs to be done in the presence of the treatment team, other offenders in the treatment group, and the offender's significant other.*

4. *Without an adequate support system to help the offender deal with the purging of the innumerable lies and egregious actions, rehabilitation is not possible.*

5. *Unless the significant other was involved in the offending itself, the complete understanding of offending behaviors and their consequences are simply overwhelming and cannot be tolerated on one's own. Support is required for the significant others to deal with numerous emotions that come with sex offender treatment, so that the significant other can be a useful resource for the treatment. This benefits both the offender and the community, who is considered at risk for future violation.*

In short, finding out that a spouse is a sex offender is incredibly difficult to deal with and it is unlikely that either party will successfully cope with it alone. If the woman can't keep it together, there's no way her partner will, which puts the community at risk due to the increased likelihood of recidivism on his part.

Clients in support groups will often say "It felt good to know that I'm not the only one with this problem," "I felt very accepted by the other members," or "It helps to be able to talk things through with people who understand, people who are struggling with this as well." The therapist or group leader's main responsibility is to facilitate group cohesiveness and disclosure to bring about the universality phenomenon. That was the mantra I adopted going forward with the women from Day 1: *Universality, universality . . .*

However, it's crucial for a group leader to possess one important attribute in order to maximize success; it's known as "credibility," and I had none. My age (twenty-five), gender (male), marital status (single), prior number of groups conducted (zero), and practical experience working with sexual offenders (none) essentially made me the worst possible person for this endeavor.

The morning of the first group I decided to play up my strengths rather than focus on my weaknesses and the poor first impression I had left with the men. I therefore engaged in an affirmation that quickly turned sour:

> *You, Rob Dobrenski, are . . . a nice person. You are fairly tall and . . . take very good care of your teeth. You're a good listener. You know the basics of human behavior and what makes people tick. Someday you might be very good at sex offender work because you've been reading about it incessantly over the past few weeks. In fact, you probably have a thousand more great qualities, but your low IQ is preventing you from thinking of any of them. What the hell is wrong with you? Shit! I'll never be successful. Why did my parents have to get divorced? It was probably my fault because of my ugly red face. Only a blind dog could ever love me. Possibly a starving cat.*

When I finished crying I thought about the first part of my speech. I decided to try my affirmation again: *I am a good listener—at least when I'm working. And I know about behavior and the dynamics of* human interaction. *If I can bring that to the table, I might be okay, and the group could thrive.*

That confidence lasted for about an hour, at which point I went back to being a shaky mess.

Like the men's group, the support group for the women also ran in an open format to parallel the work being done with the offenders. My supervisor told me that some women never left the group because they benefited from it so much and saw it as an important ritual in coping with their unusual situation. On my first night some of the women were there for the first time, but others were seasoned veterans, a similar dynamic seen in the offenders' group, with both junior and senior members. No one in the group was required to reveal the specific nature of their significant other's offense, but could if they so chose.

The idea of even introducing myself to the group terrified me to the point that I spilled coffee on my khakis. *They'll never respect me as a professional. I'm going to be laughed out of the room. I'm poor and I can't afford dry cleaning for these pants.* I went with the most generic opening possible.

"Hello, ladies. My name is Rob Dobrenski. I'm going to be leading this group for the next several months. I'm a doctoral student and I'm also working with your spouses or significant others. Maybe we could go around the room and you could introduce yourselves to me, and also mention anyone who is new to the group. Then we can talk about how we'd like to use our time together."

"I'm sorry," a woman said. "But do you mind telling us how old you are?"

Yes, I do. "I'm twenty-five years old."

"And do you have any experience in this field?" another asked.

"Not really, no. This is a training experience for me."

"I don't even know why I need to be here," said a third woman, clearly at her first session. "But if I am stuck here I'd like to make it worthwhile. Can you humor us and say how someone like you can be of help?"

I went on to tell them about what a good listener I was, my understanding of group dynamics, and my burgeoning knowledge of this particular area of psychology. Some of them looked a bit suspicious as I talked about universality and how we could all contribute to make this group a successful one. After I was done I paused, waiting for one of them to take out a large rifle and shoot me, ending my miserable existence.

"Okay then," one woman said. "This isn't a job interview, and I personally would like to make my time here productive. So let's get on with it and see if you can help this group. If not, we'll just fire you."

And just like that she began to talk about herself and why she was there. The other women followed suit. And at that moment a reality set in: The women weren't too concerned about me, my schooling, my expertise, or the stains on my pants. They were justifiably wrapped up in the chaos of their own lives. They just wanted me to lead the group to the best of my abilities. I had been so hyper-focused on what they thought of me, all of which was horrible in my own head. It was like a reverse narcissism, or something one might see in social phobia. *They are all looking at me. I'm being judged. They will see I'm weak.* Once I got out of that mind-set and allowed my thoughts to shift with an almost-audible click—once I realized that I could stop the self-serving, albeit negative, thoughts—I was able to focus on the task at hand. I still had little to no clue about what I was doing, but at least I could concentrate on learning and helping, which was why I'd been sent there in the first place.

Each week, I'd see both the offenders and their spouses in their respective groups. Many of the men associated with each other outside of group, having cigarettes or coffee in the parking lot before session. I often wondered if they actually began discussing issues at that time, because sometimes confrontations such as the one that follows would begin immediately when the members took their seats:

Junior: *Look, the kid is fifteen, but he could have said no. He wanted to do it just as much as I did. It's not fair that I have to put up with this from all of you.*

Senior: *Fuck you, you piece of shit! The state of Michigan has something called a Law of Consent, which is eighteen, asshole! And remember a simple little concept that we talked about, called PMS*? Well you have it big-time, little man!*

Wow, well put, I thought. This senior really seemed to embrace his role as a leader, and he isn't going to let new members get away with projecting the blame onto the victim. He's going to make everyone accountable for their actions, and I need to do the same thing.

Cotherapist: *Okay, you have to remember this point, and we are going to keep going over it until it sticks. Consent is eighteen—period. I understand that it is an arbitrary number, but that is how society works. As we've discussed, below that age, most are unable to process sexual relations the same way adults can. Their bodies are prepared for sex but their minds aren't nearly as sophisticated. You have to understand this, and take it in. We're here to help each other understand these points, and to make sure we follow them.*

What made working with the men particularly difficult at the start was that I didn't truly understand the psychological underpinnings of their disorder. Obviously one of the goals of the group was to prevent recidivism, but that wasn't all. We wanted to get at

---

* *PMS stood for "Poor Me Syndrome," a common phrase used to confront sex offenders.*

what *caused* these behaviors. Depression, low self-worth, the need for power or control, a lack of empathy for those who are vulnerable, being abused themselves. All of these things factored into the equation. Yet many people have these issues and do not become sexual offenders. What made these men react in this particular way? The reality was that I didn't know, and I still don't. Sadly, neither does anyone else. As with so many other disorders, the field of mental health doesn't have the means to break down all the factors into neat and clean percentages.

Because group therapy needed to be more than "Here are the rules of society—now how do we follow them?," we dug deeper. We discussed the "psychology of offending."

"Remember that our thoughts drive our actions, Rob," my cotherapist would constantly remind me. "They *think* differently, at least at first, about what they are doing. It can take years for some to see that sexual deviancy is *directly* hurting another person. That is what makes it so offensive to the public, and even the most skilled clinicians forget this important point. But if you can help these men to see how their thoughts lead to their undesirable behavior, you'll be serving both them and the community."

All of the men used a workbook to help them understand their own problems. In it they were asked to write down the thoughts and feelings they experienced before the offense, during, and after. The workbook also described how their actions could cause any number of psychological issues for their victims, such as depression, low self-esteem, and deviant sexual behavior. The members' homework included recording any triggers that inspired sexual arousal (for example, driving past a school playground), as well as any other thoughts or feelings they had experienced during the time between sessions. The goal was to get the offender to recognize connections between what was taking place in his environment and what he was thinking, which ultimately affected his feelings and behavior. One of my jobs was to review the homework and detect patterns the group members might miss, and then pass on strategies for either avoiding the triggers or coping with the impulses they aroused.

Dan was one of the seniors in the Monday-evening group, but since he was developmentally handicapped he had difficulty processing and remembering much of what we discussed during our sessions. He and I used the manual as an educational tool that helped impart lessons on how the sexual disorders afflicting these men originated. We would use the workbook to explain how offenders generally suffered from low self-esteem, had often been the victims of some form of sexual abuse during their childhood, and how their deviant sexual behavior was used to compensate for other issues, such as depression and anxiety. Because of Dan's learning disabilities, I spent extra time with him, suspecting that he would have to be closely monitored for the rest of his life. He simply did not possess the insight to understand that his actions were harmful and illegal, and this lack of self-awareness, coupled with his porous memory, led to some frustrating exchanges:

"Dan, let's see if we can summarize a little bit of our work today. Tell me more about your triggers and how they end up being so risky."

"Well, when I'm near a liquor store, that brings on the urge to drink, and when I'm drunk I want to be sexual. That's normal, though, right?"

I thought about how I used to call up Janet after a night at the bar—only to hang up before she could answer and remind me that we were through—and briefly lost focus, caught up in my own depressive nostalgia. "Let's not worry so much about what is normal; let's focus instead on what is healthy. What are some problems that come with alcohol and sex?"

"I get a hangover the next day."

"That's true. What are some other, maybe even more serious problems?"

"Hmmm . . . I guess that I have to come here where people yell at me for having sex with boys."

"That's also true. Do you remember why they yell at you?"

"Because sex is bad?"

"No, sex in and of itself isn't bad. Remember we talked about consent? And remember when we talked about all of the bad emotions young people feel when they are introduced to sex too early in life?"

"Not really. When did we do that? Can we go over it again?"

Our conversations continued in this vein for weeks. I worked from a model of "repetition and concretization." Many intellectually handicapped clients can't comprehend the abstract and the theoretical, and perspective-taking and memorizing is often quite difficult. Thus, when I became frustrated, my supervisor and cotherapist would advise me to "repeat, repeat, repeat, and keep it concrete." Eventually Dan did reach the stage where he knew he couldn't have sex with underage males. However, he never could understand why this behavior was forbidden. We were obligated to simply devise strategies that kept him away from young boys and alcohol. And although Dan would likely be considered a strong candidate to offend again, his behavior was in check according to a letter I received from my cotherapist a few years after my tenure was completed. Perhaps that will be as good as it gets.

During group, we would ask members to share their wildest sexual thoughts, and then ask the other members whether these fantasies were appropriate. The idea was to encourage fantasies in which the men engaged in mutually satisfying, consensual sex with adult partners. The revelations unveiled during this period were at times head-spinning, yet a sign that improvement was being made:

Senior: Sometimes I picture myself as a whirling dervish, and my wife is cheering me on while I work myself into a frenzy. We're both covered in chocolate, her dark and me, milk. We lick each other and when I stop to catch a breath, she beats me with a reed. Then we both climb into the bath and fondle each other until we orgasm simultaneously. That's healthy, right, Rob?

The senior's fantasy, while unorthodox, did not violate any of the conditions for what would be considered "appropriate": age, consent, and mutual satisfaction were all present. I asked my cotherapist about her reaction to this, and she agreed, while adding, "If you think those types of fantasies are just for offenders, you clearly haven't done much living."

The significant others and I met in the same large conference room as the offenders' group. It was empty save for the large table that could have easily sat twenty-five people. Because we had less than one-third of that, we scattered around the table, maybe to make the group seem larger, which would magically mean that even more people struggled from the same troubles. I always got to the room first and sat at the head of the table to establish my faux authority as the group leader. Most of the ladies would come in one at a time, except for a few veteran members who had become friends and arrived together. Most women always had at least a perfunctory smile and no visible distress. Some came in with cups of coffee, others with bottled water, and one woman even brought in cupcakes for the group. Sometimes I thought we were about to begin a book club meeting rather than talk about sex offending. In retrospect I think the women arrived still holding on to the facade they showed to the outside world: strong, put-together, functional. Some women maintained that stance throughout their time in group. "I want to be in control and I'm going to fake it till I make it."

Lengthy introductions were not required at each meeting. Instead, people just went around the room and gave their first name as a reminder to the other members. Even though my self-loathing and anxiety had mostly dissipated, I generally managed to flub even the simplest of introductions. "I'm Roberr. I mean Robert. Just Rob is fine. I'm the leader. Or facilitator. Whichever you prefer. Let's go with facilitator."

When a new member came to group, each person gave a more-detailed account of who she was and why she was here, if she so chose. The new member was then asked to say hello and share whatever information she would like.

"My name is Ann. I'm . . . not sure why I even need to be here. My husband is . . . well, he did bad things to our neighbor's daughter. He spent some time in jail and now he's home and getting . . . help here." Ann quickly became teary-eyed. "I just can't believe this has happened. My husband is a convicted sex offender. Just saying that makes me sick to my stomach. I feel horrible for the girl he did this to, and I'm so embarrassed. I don't even know what to say to her family."

She cried softly for a few moments and a group member reached for a tissue to give to her. "No!" shouted a woman I'll call Jill, a seasoned member of the group.

"What? Why not?"

"You're interrupting the healing process," she said.

Jill was right. Crying can be a form of processing, a way to make sense of everything that is happening. Most people become uncomfortable watching someone cry and will try to ease the person in distress. By doing so, they also control their own anxieties. However, it is important to let this process take its course.

Ann sniffled and said, "No, no, it's okay. I'm all right. This is just . . . hard. So hard."

"It is hard," Jill said. "We understand that here."

Many groups have their own leader outside of the facilitator. Someone tends to assume the alpha role. When not self-serving or narcissistic it can be a good thing, because this person can serve as a hybrid of therapist and client, where words of wisdom come from someone who has truly experienced what everyone in the group is going through. Jill was that person, and, while sometimes a bit rough, brought her own therapeutic element to the room.

After new members introduced themselves I reviewed the goals of the group. "Our job here is to support each other as you work through a very difficult situation. Only you know how you feel about everything that has happened to you, but hopefully the people here can share their experiences to help you make good choices and feel better about everything that has occurred. In this room no emotions are inappropriate. I hope that you will feel comfortable to share anything that is bothering you without fear of embarrassment or shame. The members of this group ideally care for each other, and it's our mission to help everyone get to a better place."

Ann raised her hand.

"Yes?"

"That was well said. Did you memorize that?"

Yes. "I review my notes periodically."

"I'll bet you have that on an index card in your pocket, Rob," Jill said with a smile. This was also true, and I went over it a half-dozen times in the bathroom prior to each start time. The ladies laughed and it was clear that many of them appreciated a lighter feel when dealing with heavy topics.

In the early weeks I found myself not saying much. New members needed to be comforted by more-senior members as they opened up. "It will get easier," "We will help you," "You're strong and you'll be okay." Although not always helpful, these words tended to stick and help the new women get acclimated, as well as begin to trust the group's cohesiveness. In fact, there were times I hardly spoke at all as the women would launch into conversations about holding one's head high in the community, or how to talk to their children about what their father had done. While all of this was going on I found myself sitting with a thought that no one had spoken: *Why did these women stay in their relationships?*

"Ladies, I need to ask you something to help me understand you better. Given what's happened to you, your family, and your relationship, why do you decide to stay with your partner? Why not just leave?"

The question came out more as a judgment than I had intended, because I wasn't necessarily thinking that every woman in the group *should* leave. I actually had no idea what anyone should do in this situation, which was part of my initial anxiety about participating in this project. Fortunately no one seemed offended by it. I suppose it was because they were used to defending their choice.

Jill spoke. "Rob, let me ask you something first: What do you think about what they've done?"

That was the question I knew I would ultimately need to answer. I remembered my supervisor's firm conviction on this issue. *It's a disorder.* As I watched the men grow as people, I believed more and more in that stance. And yet, the research on the effectiveness of "treatment" wasn't very promising. Repeat-offending rates are high. Many don't improve at all. Could that mean that their behavior was simply a conscious choice?

"I've wondered about this since I learned we'd be working together; I don't know if my answer will surprise you."

"At this point I'm getting used to surprises," Ann said, and all the ladies laughed.

"It's like . . . your husbands or loved ones have done some horrible things. They have hurt other people, possibly beyond repair. In that sense I'm really disgusted."

I waited to see or hear any reaction, but the women just looked at me and waited for me to continue.

"But I also know that many of your partners have had horrible upbringings and have a lot of psychological problems: depression, anxiety, substance abuse, and power and control issues. Whether these things are a result of what your husbands did or a cause of it, I don't know. But I don't think it's a coincidence that they coexist. Maybe if they hadn't ever engaged in deviant sexual behavior then they wouldn't have developed this obsession with it that they talk about, like the way a cocaine addict doesn't become formally addicted if he doesn't try it. But that's neither here nor there because they all did it, and now they all need treatment."

Ann pushed me a bit on this. "So what are you saying? They're ill?"

"Yes. I think they suffer from a real disorder, an illness."

There were a few suspicious glances, a few nods of agreement, and one stare into space as if deep in thought.

"You answered your own question, then," Jill said. "That's why I stay. My husband is a sick man and I'm going to stand by him."

"Well, I don't agree with that at all," another woman spoke out. "He didn't have to become a peeping tom. He chose that. He made his bed and now he has to lie in it. I'm only here to be with other people who have to cope with this. When our kids are eighteen, he's out."

"I don't know what to think," Ann said. "I flip-flop. Sometimes I think he's mentally ill, and other times I believe he's simply a monster. I was hoping this group would help me to figure out what I really know and want."

"So, Rob, since you're an active member of the group now, why don't you share with us what you would do if you were in our spot?" Jill asked.

Over time it became apparent that the women wanted to hear my personal opinions on many topics. Whether it was for my "expertise" or simply for a man's take on this problem, they clearly wanted to draw me into the discussion. Not knowing a lot about the protocol of support groups, I wasn't sure how I felt about this pull from them. When I asked Nurse Ratched about how to handle such a situation, she said simply, "Rob, tell these women the truth. Do not lie to them. If you feel uncomfortable, just say so, but don't feed them bullshit. They'll know and resent you for it. You are developing nicely as a clinician, but I want you to be more of yourself in session. Let your personality come through."

"I don't think I would stay with someone who did this," I admitted. "I don't judge anyone for their choices in this group, and as I said, I do believe it is an illness, but I'm pretty sure I couldn't handle the betrayal."

"So you'd leave someone who became schizophrenic?" Jill asked, in a way that seemed less a challenge than a way to more fully develop the discussion. "That's an illness as well."

"It is, and I would like to think that I wouldn't leave a person who developed schizophrenia. But of course I can't say for sure, because that hasn't happened to me at this point in my life."

In fact, not much at all had happened to me at that age, which is why I was completely naive to the world and sounded like an idiot when I tried to talk about anything important. "But the nature of the illnesses is different. One often involves hallucinations, and the other involves sexual activity with another person. I don't see them as fair comparison points."

"I agree," said Ann. "If my husband were schizophrenic, I don't think I'd feel this anger toward him. And if pedophilia is an illness, then okay—fine. I get it. But that doesn't change the fact that he broke our marital vows. That part doesn't change even if it's due to 'illness,' which is why I struggle with what to do going forward."

Jill spoke. "That's why you're here. I've made a choice to stay and work it out. This woman has chosen to leave when the time is right for her. Other women just leave and don't look back. We'll help you figure that out. Even Rob here seems like he could contribute to helping you with this problem, and he probably hasn't even started shaving yet."

I hoped the compliment was as true as the insult.

One night before the men's group began, my supervisor called my cotherapist and me into her office. "One of the men has offended again," she said with a very serious look.

"What? Who?" I asked.

She told me his name and that he had been arrested for having sex with a thirteen-year-old girl. And yet he had been released on bail and would be in group tonight. She gave my cotherapist a police report, detailing what the man had done and apparently the little remorse he had shown after the fact. She looked to the cotherapist. "You know what to do." My cotherapist perused the form, nodded, and took me by the arm. "Come on, Rob," she said. "This is the hard part."

When we sat down with the group, my cotherapist immediately spoke. "I need to address someone in particular." She looked at the man who had committed the crime. He looked back, unsurprised to be singled out.

"You have violated the one and only nonnegotiable rule of this group," she said. "Everyone here has been told that we can help you with anything, anything at all, as long as you don't cross that line into offending. You were not able to do that."

The man simply hung his head in what seemed to be a combination of shame and defeat.

"Unfortunately," she said, "you cannot stay in group with us anymore. The law will deal with you from now on. You've damaged another person whose life may never be the same. You betrayed your family and the members of this group who work their asses off to live a different life. Rob and I have given our best to you, and in turn we expected the best *from* you. And while you may have an illness, we expect you to take your medicine. We expected you to call us, to tell us about any urges, thoughts, and feelings you might have been having. But you did none of those things. And therefore, you will no longer be a part of this group. Now please leave."

The man didn't protest. He got up, picked up his jacket, and left, not acknowledging anyone or anything said to him. When he left I felt an urge to say something, to contribute at least a sentence.

"That was hard to watch," I said. "Does anyone else have feelings about what just happened here?"

A senior spoke. "You know, I still get urges. I haven't done anything wrong in three years. What we have is an addiction of sorts, but I control it. I'm faithful to my wife now, I don't put myself in risky situations, and I come to group and do my homework. I hope that guy ultimately changes, but the people here, right now, have to rally together and stay focused."

At that moment, my cotherapist spoke. "You are right. We need to press on, because there are men here who want to get better."

As the weeks went on, with me at the helm, the women's group started to develop a positive routine. We tried our best to answer very difficult questions: Why did their husbands do this? How could they have risked losing everything: their family, their jobs, and their freedom? What does it mean that they are "sick"? And what about the victims? How would their lives be altered? While we never developed definitive answers, our discussions continued to bring the women closer together.

The group members would give advice to each other. They continued to ask for my opinions. They never overtly hated me for being a man, as my supervisor had suggested they might. We talked about how the women could handle themselves in the community. We discussed how to cope with the gamut of emotions that comes along with this new life that they now needed to live. We even talked about their sex lives. Sometimes people in the group would cry, sometimes they would get angry, and other times they would make jokes, often at my expense:

"My husband and I try to be sexual, but after all that's happened, I can't relax, and of course I can't have an orgasm. I'm not sure how to talk to him about this. Rob, your girlfriends probably complain all the time about not having orgasms with you. How do you handle such criticism?"

One woman brought in a small bag of sex toys for the women to examine, just in case they wanted to "go it alone for a while," according to the woman. "Let's see if Rob knows what each of these wonderful pieces of technology do!"

After a few months the group membership reached a plateau. While new women had come in to the group, a small number of others had decided they were leaving their partners, and didn't need the group's support any longer. This position was never challenged, and members were told that the door was always open if they changed their minds about needing help.

With a set number of eight people, we continued to work on ways of coping with this new life that the women hadn't asked for. Week after week the women gave each other powerful support, and they changed because of it. You could see them grow as people. They became empowered. They processed what had happened to them through talk and reflection. Sometimes the women would bring in letters that they had written to their partners. The women would read them aloud and talk about the feelings of anger, betrayal, embarrassment, and sometimes empathy they felt toward their partner's illness. They would read, cry, yell, and usually say they felt better because of it—not only because of the catharsis but also because they were not judged for any of their thoughts or feelings. Sometimes the women gave the letters to their husbands; other times, they simply wanted to express what they felt in a safe forum.

The woman whose husband had had sex with the thirteen-year-old girl decided to stay in group. "I'm leaving him," she said. "He is sick—I truly believe that—but I myself need this group. I need . . . you," she said, and tears began to trickle down her face. Three of the women almost leapt out of their chairs to hug her, stroke her hair, and tell her "You'll be okay, you'll be okay . . ." And, with the help of the group, the woman was determined to prove them right.

Sometimes the women wrote letters to the victims, apologizing for their partners' actions and saying that if they had known, if they had only known that something like this could happen, they would have stopped it. The group members focused on reducing guilt about being powerless to stop such actions by being empathic and pushing each other to be kind to themselves. Again, no judgments.

What ultimately developed was a grieving process: the loss of the life they had once had, and what they thought their lives would be going forward. When the women embraced this fact—that their husbands were not the people they once thought they were . . . that life was different, but certainly not over—the women changed as well.

When springtime came I was ready to complete my internship, and would be leaving the group soon. That meant saying good-bye to the women I had spent each week with for almost a full year. I thought a lot about whether or not my absence would be disruptive, as many people develop intense attachments to their therapists. If Carol had suspended her practice while I was in crisis, my world would have imploded. I felt as if I literally *needed* her, and that's something mental health professionals have to get comfortable with if they want to do this job.

The men's group continued while I started to wrap up my tenure. At one session, we watched videos which showed a sexual abuse victim asking questions to a panel of offenders. The offenders hadn't violated her specifically, but they were symbolic of the person who had betrayed her. She would posit questions to help her gain clarity, and they would answer her in a supposedly truthful way.

"Do you know how my life is different now?" she asked.

"I didn't, but I do now," one man answered. "Maybe at the time I thought about it a bit, but I didn't care. I just had an urge and it needed to be filled."

"Were any of you ever sexually assaulted?" she asked.

Some of the men raised their hands; others did not.

"Was it just about the sex for you?" she asked.

"No, not for me. I'd say 5 percent was about sex. The rest was trying to feel important, in control. I still don't understand that and probably never will. But I work hard every day to not fuck up anyone else."

The videos were designed to develop empathy in our group members. While some new members scoffed at the simplicity of the exchange, others cried while watching, and some shook their heads in shame at what they had done. It was a helpful exercise for most.

When men reach the end stages of sex therapy, they write letters to their victims. Mailing the letters would violate their parole or treatment, so the intended recipients never actually see them, but that was irrelevant to the exercise. Just the act of recording their thoughts and feelings toward the person they had violated often led to a coalescence of everything the offender had learned during his tenure Up North. Like a large portion of the general public, many clinicians believe sexual offenders simply "are what they are"—that they can't be changed, and that society would be better off locking them away forever. If one reviews the latest research on sex offender treatment, there would be spotty results to support positive outcomes, so it is not easy to argue against the antitherapy lobby. However, after my experience with these men, when I heard some offenders read their letters out loud, the emotion in their voices and the insights contained in their words, I sometimes felt hope. Here is one example:

Dear Joanne,

As part of my rehabilitation program, I am writing to apologize for what I did to you. I have been in treatment for three years now, every week. I am not the same person that did those horrible things to you.

I know now why I did what I did. I didn't value myself as a person, and I didn't value others. I was, and still am, depressed, but I don't view things as hopeless as they once were. I used sex with girls to feel better about myself, to feel like a man. I picked younger girls to be with me because I didn't believe that an adult would want me. Sex covered up my depression, at least for a little while, but at a terrible expense to you. I know that I have damaged your self-esteem, made you feel vulnerable and unsafe. I often wonder if you see yourself as "damaged goods" because of me. I don't doubt that my actions have caused you to have trust issues, body image issues, nightmares, and other horrible, horrible emotions.

After I got caught doing those things to you, I could only focus on myself. I labeled myself as a victim. I knew that I would lose my job and my family, and that I was looking at possible prison time. All of that did, in fact, happen.

When I got out, they sent me here, to the sexual rehabilitation center. For months, I continued to see myself as the victim, not you. I saw myself as broken: alone, no job, and forever branded a pedophile. Every day I thought about leaving this place, killing myself. Eating, trying to sleep, reading, doing my therapy homework, all the time I thought about simply doing myself in. Then one day I felt this incredible, amazing, and painful guilt. I started to think about YOU, what all this meant in YOUR world. And the suicidal thoughts went away. I started thinking of ways to make amends, to take back what I did, to make you feel better.

Unfortunately, I can't take back what I did. My therapists here, though, told me that I can try to express how sorry I am, that I can learn more about WHY I did what I did, and how to prevent it in the future. They told me that I can help others, people like yourself, maybe by showing you ways to protect yourself from offenders. And I can work with other offenders to help them not hurt people anymore. Knowing this made me want to go on with life, to be a productive member of society, not some delinquent fuck-up who destroys people's lives.

Joanne, I hope you will recognize that there are good people in the world, people who aren't like me. Not everyone will do those things to you, violate you and take away your youth and innocence like I did. There are truly decent people out there, and I'm trying to become one of them. I will never be able to be around children the way other adults can, but I will always work with my counselor to make good choices and appropriate decisions. I will help others to prevent these things from happening again. That is the best I can do. I can't take away what I did. I wish I could. Joanne, I'm sorry I'm sorry, I'm so sorry . . .

Having read the letter aloud to the group, the senior was sobbing. Other members patted him on the back; someone had held his hand as he struggled through the conclusion. This is a rite of passage in treatment. In theory, once they've completed the letters, they have completed a dark chapter in their lives. After that session, this particular senior was allowed to gradually taper off his attendance in group. Today he gives lectures on the nature of sexual offenses throughout his community, and he is considered a model client for the group.

With the odds against recovery being long, the treatment can still be worthwhile because it can pull at least some offenders away from their deviant behavior. Illness or not, biology in and of itself cannot explain away the work we had done.

When I was done with my nine-month tour of duty, one member went out of his way to thank me: "You didn't come here judging us as monsters or outcasts. You listened to us for a long time before finally speaking, and a lot of what you said helped to guide us in the right direction, helped us to make a good choice for that particular day. You made us more aware of others, less focused on ourselves. You changed our lives for the better."

I knew Nurse Ratched would be proud when I recited that back to her. But what made this ending bittersweet was not only that I'd never see these men again, but that I'd also be saying good-bye to their wives as well. I was leaving not just one client, like I'd see in traditional therapy, but rather a group of families.

My time in this group had been preset from the day I'd walked through the agency's door: September to May. But when May came, I didn't like the idea of leaving. After such an unusual and intense training experience, the thought of going back to doing research on Rorschach tests wasn't overly appealing. With the groups it felt like I was doing real work, but more importantly, I knew that I would miss a lot of the people in the treatment program.

Shrinks who say they love or even like all their clients are either delusional or lying. Not everyone who comes into therapy is likable, and often their psychological problems can make them very difficult to deal with. Other times people are just disagreeable. Make no mistake: There isn't a shrink who is going to be a perfect fit for every client, and indeed, certain clients will actively dislike their therapists. That being said, I was fortunate in this particular situation because I did like many of the men and women there, and the feeling appeared to be mutual.

Even though our support group wasn't a formal therapy setting, many of the women improved to the point that they didn't need the group anymore (assuming their significant others were no longer in treatment, either through graduation or from being removed due to recidivism). Others reported that they would stay in the group for as long as it existed, that they always took something new from what their fellow members had to say. Some of the women saw themselves as role models for new members and relished the opportunity to serve as a sponsor of sorts for new participants.

For the last group I had a small speech planned: I'd review what we'd learned together, tell them how proud I was of them, and that they should never stop growing, rah rah rah! I'd never successfully delivered a predetermined speech and I knew this would be no exception, so I scrapped it before group and decided to let the final session flow organically.

Nurse Ratched had some charts and notes for me to sign before I left the agency for the last time. "I wouldn't be a supervisor without being a hard-ass now, would I?" she asked. "So you have to do some paperwork." At the bottom of all the charts was a card from her, blank on the front. On the inside it simply said, "You came in here as a boy and are leaving as a man. You will be a great psychologist one day, Mr. Dobrenski, and I'd like to believe I'm a part of that. Never stop learning, and never run from what is different and scary."

After I'd read it, Nurse Ratched tapped me on the shoulder, stuck out her hand for a shake, and said, "Now go finish up your last group with your ladies."

I arrived a few minutes late to find the women already there, talking up a storm.

"He did *what?* That's horrible."

"He should be lynched for that."

"String him up by his balls!"

"Hi, ladies," I said. "I think I'm missing an interesting conversation here."

"Jill's husband was late for their anniversary dinner. Being *late* is something we don't tolerate around here," Anne said with a wink.

"Ah, my supervisor warned me about negative reactions toward me. This is because I'm a man?"

"Yep. You're all the same," Jill said.

"Fortunately, not everyone is like our men," Anne said with a small frown.

"No, not everyone is like that," I said. "You all have a very unique situation."

We talked about this notion of "being different." Some women challenged the idea, stating that plenty of people have family members who are murderers, thieves, rapists, or even a combination of those things. "No one has a perfect family," one woman asserted. "People are messed up, they do messed-up things. Sometimes *really* messed-up things. Do you know how many thousands upon thousands of people are in prison? Well, those people have families. That's us."

Others held fast to the idea that the lives of the women in this group weren't like anyone else's. "I don't know anyone who is married to a pedophile," said Ann. "I know these people exist, but when I picture them, they're just hypothetical figures, blank faces on generic bodies. So it's only here that I feel I'm with my own kind."

"That's why I'm here, and I'll probably never leave. Because we're different," Jill said. "However, this one," she said, pointing at me, "is leaving us." She smiled.

I couldn't help but think there was at least a little resentment behind that.

"Yes, as we've discussed, today is the day," I said. "I'd like to ask each of you how you feel about this."

"And are you going to share as well?" one woman asked.

"Absolutely."

Jill spoke. "I have mixed feelings about this. Our last two group leaders were women, so this is a new experience for me." She paused and looked down into her lap. "I'm happy for you in some ways. You've taken another step toward getting your PhD. You probably learned a lot between working with us and our partners, and you were helpful, and I'm grateful for that."

"Thank you," I said.

"But part of me is very jealous. You get to leave here, and when you do your life is your own. We have to remain the 'significant others of sex offenders,' and you don't have to carry that burden. I resent that, and I feel like you're abandoning us."

We had spent a small number of sessions talking about how the women might feel about me leaving. This is always good clinical practice but not always easy to implement, especially in groups. The members have crises and problems to attend to, and not everyone is comfortable sharing thoughts about their group leader. So this was our first foray into deep feelings about . . . termination.

"Do other people feel this way?" I asked.

One woman nodded, and then Ann spoke. "I feel abandoned but I don't resent you or feel jealous. I'll just miss you."

"I wouldn't blame anyone for feeling resentful or abandoned," I said. "This is how the system works, and unfortunately, people come and go through this revolving door that is our lives." It wasn't my goal to become a walking cliché that evening, but there you have it.

"I want you to know," I continued, "that I will miss this group terribly. You've all been through a lot, and those of you sitting here decided to fight back against your problems. Even if that meant leaving your spouse, you didn't bail and hide under a rock. You sat here, week after week, and worked through the feelings. I'd like to think I helped with that. I didn't always agree with your decisions, but to say I respect you for your work is an understatement."

"Well, we respect you too, soon-to-be Dr. Rob," said Ann. "And I'll bet you'll make a lady very happy someday with all of the knowledge about sex you learned from our discussions."

At the end of the session the ladies gave me a card. It had a small tree on the front. Inside it had all of their signatures scattered about, and, in the middle, it said:

STAY WARM

STAY SAFE

AND FOR GOD'S SAKE, STAY LEGAL!

They all laughed as I read the card aloud, and I gave a small smile. Even though the women knew I was not flawless, Freud might have said that, in addition to using humor to protect against psychological pain, the last line was a warning to not shatter the positive image they had of me. This isn't unheard of in therapy, where clients will give admonishments and pieces of advice that underneath the surface are really saying, "Please don't change; don't become something bad. I need you to stay exactly who you are!"

And just like that it was over. Some women gave me a hug good-bye; others simply waved as they walked out. The next week a new intern would be in my spot, doing my job and forming a relationship with the men and women in the groups. *My* men and women. I was jealous that someone else was going to be helping them from this point forward.

That was my first experience with the "loss" involved in a therapeutic relationship, at least of one that had some significant time behind it. Even today this part of the job doesn't get much easier. The best therapy relationships are the ones that are hard to let go of, even when you're ecstatic for the person who has made the gains they sought out.

I left the agency that night and met up with my fellow students, many of whom had finished their internships as well. We were that much closer to graduation. One year to go. We drank beer and wine and partied to start off the summer. But for a few weeks after I'd left, I had a nagging feeling that I can only describe as grief. All of us grew as people because of our experiences together, but I still lost them and they'd lost me. I eventually processed those feelings and moved on to other groups and other therapy relationships— but I will always remember these particular men and women in a very unique way.

Epilogue:
Cured?

Clients will sometimes ask when it's time to end therapy or stop medication. This is often a very difficult question to answer. Because life is so fluid—changes in serotonin levels, altered life circumstances, therapy techniques that improve coping skills, etc.—it can be hard to determine when and if a client is "done." Depending on the nature of the condition, some clients need to take medication and be in therapy for their entire lives, while others are engaged for only a few weeks or months. And most shrinks agree that decisions like these have a certain trial-and-error approach: "Let's try decreasing your medication and/or tapering off your therapy, and we'll see what happens. If you begin to feel worse, we'll start up again."

Sometimes, however, you simply know that you've completed your work. Deb and Sara knew. So did Bill. And one day I woke up and I knew as well. I called my psychiatrist and told him that I wanted to come off the Zoloft. Even though I was only a graduate student, he talked to me as if I was a peer.

"How long have you been asymptomatic now?" he asked.

"At least three months, maybe more. I'm ready."

"Okay, taper down to twenty-five milligrams for three days, then to ten for two days, and you're done. Call me if you need anything," he said.

"I will. Thank you."

"Good luck, Rob. I don't think I'll be seeing you again."

"Let's hope not," I said, and hung up.

When I went to therapy the following week the Zoloft was out of my system. I felt good. "I think I'm ready to end therapy—at least for now."

Carol didn't look surprised. She had hinted a few weeks prior that I might be getting ready to wrap up. Our most recent sessions had involved me reviewing events of my week, but not reporting many "problems." There were also times that I had little to say at all. For me that meant I was ready to pack it in.

"Do you want to consider exploring other areas of your life?" she asked. "We talked so much about Janet. Anything else on your plate?"

"I suppose there's always something, but nothing is really pressing right now," I said. "I'm sure if we explored every avenue of my life we'd come up with material, but for right now I'd just like to ride the wave of feeling good. I'll be back when I need to be."

Carol smiled. "It's not all that often I get to work with a peer-in-the-making. This was a real treat."

I quickly thought about how far I had come in the months prior. From unsolicited crying spells and blazing jealousy and horrible sleep and Beer and Tears to a previously unfathomable greater sense of self-control. I felt healthy. I can't definitively say that I would not have gotten through it without Carol; people experience loss every day and somehow manage. But at that moment, it seemed like Carol had been a godsend. She had picked me up and carried me across raging rivers and hot coals, whispering *You'll be okay, you'll be okay* throughout the entire journey.

"I can't even begin to tell you how thankful I am. I'm going to miss coming here."

"I'll miss that, too. Remember what we talked about and you'll be fine. You know where to find me."

And that was that. We both stood up, she shook my hand as she had the day we met, gave me a warm smile, and opened the office door. And that was the last time I saw Carol, because I graduated soon after and moved to another part of the country.

Whenever I apply any of the tools she taught me, though, I think about her and wonder how she is, who she's helped. I wonder if she thinks about me and how I'm doing. But the nature of the shrink-patient relationship is simple: When it's over, that's it. Save for a possible e-mail down the line to say hello, or the off chance you'll bump into each other at the grocery store (Dr. Pete's worst nightmare), you both leave each other's lives, often permanently.

I thought about how lucky I was to be "cured," and about my own patients' outcomes. For Bill, driving that car dissolved his depression, which was why he was there with me in the first place. He wasn't looking to become the most insightful, cerebral person in the world, nor was he required to. He wanted to be free of his misery and he achieved that. Sara was similar. She needed to gain closure on the death of her husband. Once that happened, she too was ready to move on with her life. She wasn't obligated to process her feelings every week, without fail, in the office with me (and some would argue that this wouldn't be a wise choice anyway). She needed to see that a life without her husband was more than an intellectual discussion; it needed to be a reality. And when it was, she needed to go out and actually live it.

Scott needed to recognize that the family he so craved was actually right in front of him. Jim's task was to stop viewing himself as weak simply because he was a doctor with a mental illness. Jack needed to step into a young man's shoes and begin his first steps toward becoming a complete person, not just a precocious walking dictionary. And Deb needed to learn how to control her own thoughts when she was reminded of her trauma.

I could have simply told all of these people what I thoroughly believed they needed. In fact, many of their friends and family had already done that. That's what makes therapy such a fascinating journey; it allows you to discover something about yourself, *for* yourself. The therapist is simply a conduit to that insight and knowledge. Like Carol did for me, a therapist may give you the tools to help counter maladaptive thinking; provide tips on how to slow down your heart rate during a panic attack; or teach couples how not to throw each other out of a twenty-story window. A therapist earns his living through simply *facilitating* change—by being along for the ride.

While there are dozens upon dozens of therapeutic approaches, they tend to share certain characteristics: They help the client to feel both validated and accepted; they give the client a platform and framework in which to discuss problems; they help clients to see that the way they are currently viewing their world is not in their best interests; and, sometimes, they give the client a set of skills to help counter the mind-set that is holding them back from a more productive, happier life. Various schools of thought will frame these basic principles in different ways, but when the subtleties of the approaches are boiled down, these are the basic elements in the therapy room.

For people like Elaine, David, and, of course, Dr. Pete, positive outcomes are not likely. Does that mean they should cease their treatments? Absolutely not. The medications and therapy are likely helping them to some degree, and the risk would be that they could all completely decompensate without some form of intervention. But a full, complete, and high-quality life is not in the cards for these people, at least not with the system of mental health that we have right now. Something new and radical will need to come along, and that's not going to happen anytime soon, most likely not in my lifetime.

As for me, do I still miss Janet? Not at all. It wasn't *her* per se that I wanted. Do I still grapple with loss, especially within romantic relationships? Definitely. Is jealousy—at least the kind that sits in my head and treats it like a personal playground—still a problem?

Sometimes. And do I push people away at times because I antici-pate getting hurt? Yes. And that's why I periodically go to therapy now—to continue to make sense of and, ultimately, to eliminate those problems. It may take many more years, but I do hope to get there one day.

The day I stepped out of Carol's office and the door closed behind me, I saw a middle-aged man in the waiting room wear-ing a very expensive suit—most likely a businessman. He looked very nervous, gripping a copy of *Harper's* hard in both hands. I wondered what his pain must be like, if he was embarrassed about being there, if he knew what to expect from Carol. I resisted an urge to share something with him.

Don't worry, you're in good hands with Carol. And don't sweat the fact that you're seeing a shrink. You probably don't know it yet, but more people like you and me should be getting help. In fact, I'll let you in on a little secret, one I wish I knew years ago: at some point in our lives, to one degree or another, we're all crazy.

Acknowledgments

No one deserves more thanks than Ben Corman at Attention Crash.Net. A great writer and friend, he taught me everything I know about writing and telling a story. If there hadn't been a special group of people already in mind, this book would have been dedicated to him. Given such tutelage, if this book was a bad read, consider it his fault.

Thank you to Holly Rubino and everyone at Lyons Press, my agent Jon Sternfeld, Jack, Tucker, PJ, Donika, Mark, Jenna, Skip, Moira, Craig, Lucy, Dick, Lauren Galit, BL1Y.com, Gina, Becky, Luke, everyone at Rudius Media, my "reading group" who gave me great feedback as the book was in early development, Kevin, Michelle, Catherine, Paul, Dan, Dreams, Big Marc, Chater, Christopher, the Writing Group, every professor who taught me how to do my job, every client who has walked through the door, all of my friends who read countless blog posts and book drafts that were so awful they will never be seen again, every colleague who told me that I would fail and had no business writing about our jobs, the shrinks who wouldn't let me work in their practices because I doubled as a writer with a "far too honest take on our field," and all the readers at ShrinkTalk.Net who took time out of their schedules to look at my material. You all gave me motivation to write this.

Thank you, Robin. You pushed me to be a better person, to not resign myself to what I thought I could only be.

Thank you, Mom and Dad. I'd be nowhere without you both.

Thank you, Lidia. You're my biggest and most important fan.

About the Author

Dr. Rob Dobrenski received his B.A. from Rutgers University and his Master of Arts and PhD in Clinical Psychology at the University of Toledo. He completed his post-doctoral fellowship at Cornell Medical Center/ New York Hospital, and he currently works in private practice in New York City.

Rob is the founder/author of the popular website, ShrinkTalk .Net. You can also find his work in *The Best Creative Nonfiction, Volume 2*, edited by Lee Gutkind.